THE SPIRIT OF THE REVOLUTION

KENNIKAT AMERICAN BICENTENNIAL SERIES
Under the General Editorial Supervision of
Dr. Ralph Adams Brown
Professor of History, State University of New York

LAFAYETTE

THE SPIRIT OF THE REVOLUTION

New Light from Some of the Original Sources of American History

BY

JOHN C. FITZPATRICK, A.M.

ASSISTANT CHIEF, MANUSCRIPT DIVISION, LIBRARY OF CONGRESS

WITH ILLUSTRATIONS

KENNIKAT PRESS
Port Washington, N. Y./London

134300

First published in 1924
Reissued in 1970 by Kennikat Press
Library of Congress Catalog Card No: 71-120875
ISBN 0-8046-1268-4

Manufactured by Taylor Publishing Company   Dallas, Texas

KENNIKAT AMERICAN BICENTENNIAL SERIES

PREFACE

THE main facts and broad outlines of our beginnings as a Nation are well established and plainly set forth in easily accessible print. The details of the WHY and HOW are not always so plainly recorded, nor readily found, and it was to furnish answers to some of the WHY'S and HOW'S that these articles were written.

The three papers on the Declaration of Independence contain considerable new and not easily obtainable information respecting that immortal document; those on the origin of the symbols U.S. and U.S.A., the Post-Office of the Revolution, and the Medal of Honor of the Continental Army, and the papers touching upon George Washington serve to illustrate the many existing possibilities to be developed by an intensive scrutiny of the original sources of our American history.

The material for all of the articles has been drawn, in the main, from that vast body of historical manuscripts preserved in the Library of Congress and, to the greatest extent, from the half a thousand volumes of the Papers of the Continental Congress, the four hundred or more volumes of those of George Washington, and the two hundred and fifty or so volumes of Thomas Jefferson.

The original form of publication of these sketches precluded the citation of authorities, and criticism is deliberately risked in the present instance by omitting footnote references which, however proper and desirable in a monograph, are not absolutely necessary in less exhaustive papers the main purpose of which is to picture some of the color and fire of the times that tried men's souls in America. If through such historical details as are here given we catch a glimpse of the spark and glow of the spirit of the Revolution, it will aid in securing for us a firmer foundation for the understanding of our United States of to-day.

WASHINGTON, D.C.

For permission to use these papers grateful acknowledgment is made to the Daughters of the American Revolution Magazine and to its capable editor, Miss Natalie Sumner Lincoln.

CONTENTS

CONTENTS

ILLUSTRATIONS

*The facsimiles of documents are all from the
original manuscripts in the Library of Congress*

THE SPIRIT OF THE REVOLUTION

I

THE MANUSCRIPT FROM WHICH JEFFERSON WROTE THE DECLARATION OF INDEPENDENCE

THE story of the writing of the Declaration of Independence usually begins with what is called the first draft of that immortal document, in the handwriting of Thomas Jefferson, which was submitted to Congress, June 28, 1776, as the report of the committee appointed June 11th to draft a declaration. Few people know that there is, in the Jefferson Papers, in the Library of Congress, a practically unknown manuscript, which is the very first arraignment of the charges of tyranny against the British king, and from which Jefferson wrote the Declaration of Independence.

It is a six-page, folio document, entirely in Jefferson's handwriting and endorsed by him:

Constitution of Virginia first ideas of
Th: J. communicated to a member
of the Convention:

The first page of this manuscript is in the form of a preamble, or series of reasons why Virginia repudiates her allegiance to George III and establishes for herself a constitution of her own making. This manuscript has remained in its undeserved seclusion through one of those curious misadventures which usually end in the loss or destruction of the papers, and which, unhappily, are all too frequent with our valuable governmental records. That this paper survived was a fact unknown until comparatively recently, and now that this draft has been repaired and safely protected against all future accident it should be given its proper place among the truly great historical manuscripts of American history.

The date of the creation of this paper lies somewhere between May 27th and June 10, 1776, before the appointment, by Congress, of the committee to draft the Declaration. A copy of it was sent by the hand of George Wythe to Edmund Pendleton, the President of the Virginia Convention. By the time Wythe reached Williamsburg, a constitution had been decided upon, so this Jefferson plan arrived too late. The Convention liked his Preamble, however, prefaced its constitution with it, and adopted the whole on May 29, 1776.

The Declaration of Independence is blood brother to the Virginia Constitution and the Bill of Rights of 1776. Its genesis, roughly speaking, is the first three sections of George Mason's immortal composition, Thomas Jefferson's Preamble to the Virginia Constitution, and Richard Henry Lee's resolution of independence which the Virginia Convention had directed its delegates in the Continental Congress to introduce. The first three sections of Mason's Bill of Rights are easily recognized in Jefferson's polished condensation in the third, fourth, fifth, and sixth lines of the original, signed Declaration:

1. All men are by nature equally free and independent and have certain inherent rights, of which ... they cannot by any compact, deprive or divest their posterity; namely, the enjoyment of life and liberty ... and pursuing and obtaining happiness and safety.

2. That all power is vested in, and consequently derived from the people. ...

3. That government is, or ought to be, instituted for the common benefit, protection, and security of the people, nation, or community; ... when any government shall be found inadequate or contrary to these purposes, a majority of the community hath an indubitable, inalienable, and indefeasible right to reform, alter, or abolish it...

Jefferson's Preamble, or charges of tyranny against King George, come next, and lastly, Lee's resolution is incorporated, word for word, as the finish and climax.

The Declaration of Independence thus is a Virginia product, for George Mason's Bill of Rights was adopted June 12, 1776; Jefferson's Preamble was adopted (with the Constitution) May 29th, and Lee's resolution of independence closely approximates the language of Virginia's resolutions of independence which were passed by the Convention May 15th, the authorship of which rests jointly in Patrick Henry,

Thomas Nelson, Edmund Pendleton and Meriwether Smith.

Now let us take a brief survey of the situation: Some time between May 27th, when Jefferson, in Philadelphia, first learned of Virginia's intention to break with Britain and form a new constitution, and June 10th, he composed a plan of government, or constitution, for his native State. On June 7, 1776, acting upon the instructions received, Richard Henry Lee moved, in the Continental Congress, "That these United Colonies are, and of right ought to be, free and independent States, that they are absolved from all allegiance to the British Crown, and that all political connection between them and the State of Great Britain is, and ought to be, totally dissolved." This motion was heatedly debated for nearly a month, but from the first it was apparent that eventually it would be adopted. It would be the great and final casting of the die of separation, and Congress felt that a form of announcement of that step would be needed that would be more impressive, more of an attention riveting manifesto, than the short and concise wording of Lee's resolution would present. In anticipation of the adoption of the resolution Congress appointed, on June 11, 1776, a committee to prepare such a form of announcement, or declaration, of the expected assumption of independence. This committee, composed of Jefferson, John Adams, Benjamin Franklin, Robert R. Livingston and Roger Sherman, met on that same day for the first time, to plan a declaration. How the composition of the document was entrusted by the committee to Jefferson and Adams and by the latter entirely to the former is not of great moment here. It was so left, and Jefferson found himself confronted with a task precisely similar to the one he had voluntarily set himself but two weeks before. Then he had planned a series of reasons, justifying to the world the breaking of Virginia's political association with Great Britain, and followed it with his plan for a new government; now he was to justify the breaking of the political bands binding the Colonies to Britain, and to follow that justification with the formally adopted resolution (Lee's) of independence. There is no doubt of his action. The ink was scarcely dry upon his plan for Virginia's constitution; John Adams says: "We were all in haste; Congress was impatient . . ." With this manuscript draft of the Preamble before him, Jefferson copied off its charges of tyranny against the king.

There are sixteen numbered charges in the Preamble, subdivided into twenty-three separate reasons why the Colony of Virginia considered herself no longer under the allegiance of George III. Some alterations, of course, were made, and the twenty-three of the Preamble became the twenty-eight of the Declaration by the addition of three new indictments and the expansion of the sixth of the Preamble into the eighth, ninth, and tenth of the Declaration. The exact order of the accusations in the Preamble is altered but twice in the Declaration, and, of the twenty-eight reasons in the Declaration for the assumption of independence, but three are missing from the Preamble and only one of the Preamble's twenty-three is missing from the Declaration. This one, the accusation of inciting slave insurrections, and of preventing the Colonies from checking the growth of slavery, was in the draft of the Declaration submitted to Congress. It was suppressed by that body, but a hint of it remains in the twenty-seventh of the Declaration's charges: "He has excited domestic insurrections amongst us."

While at work in committee upon the revision of the Preamble to suit the new need, a copy of the Virginia Bill of Rights, as adopted, reached Jefferson through the public prints. The clarion note of liberty in its first three sections found sympathetic echo in his brain; he seized upon them and, with the artist's perfect judgment, commenced the Declaration with the trumpet blast of their bold principles; the revised Preamble followed, and, after that, Lee's resolution was written in to close the achievement. The draft of this completed effort was finally agreed to in committee and submitted to Congress four days before the passage of Lee's resolution. It was laid on the table until that resolution could be disposed of, and, on July 1st, Congress for the first time gave consideration to it. On July 2d, Lee's resolution was adopted,

FIRST PAGE OF A DRAFT OF THE DECLARATION OF INDEPENDENCE IN THE HANDWRITING OF THOMAS JEFFERSON

and immediately thereafter Jefferson's draft of the Declaration was taken up as unfinished business in the committee of the whole. Some changes were made, the most drastic being the suppression, as before stated, of the noble principle involved in the charge of not allowing the Colonies to stop the slave trade, and, on July 4, 1776, George Mason's theory of liberty, Jefferson's Preamble to the Virginia Constitution, and Richard Henry Lee's resolution of independence were agreed to by Congress as the form of the announcement that the United Colonies had, on July 2d, become free and independent States. July 2, 1776, is the day upon which the United States became a nation, and on July 4th we declared "to a candid world" the action taken on July 2d.

The genius of Jefferson and his high literary skill nowhere show to better advantage than in this work of fusing together in the Declaration of Independence the three basic elements noted. As revised in the Declaration the Preamble is smoother, clearer, and more forceful. Edmund Pendleton wrote to Jefferson on July 22, 1776, after reading the Declaration for the first time: "I expected you had in the preamble to our form of Government [the Virginia Constitution], exhausted the subject of complaint against George III, and was at a loss to discover what the Congress would do for one to their Declaration of Independence without copying, but find you have acquitted yourselves very well on that score."

The Declaration was not signed on July 4, 1776.
The evidence as to this is overwhelming and complete. It was first published in printed form and these
printed copies, or broadsides as they are called, were
set up and run off from the press of John Dunlap,
printer to Congress, during the night of July 4th.
They were ready for distribution the next day, July
5th. The engrossing and signing appear to be something of an afterthought. The important step was the
assumption of independence; that being taken and the
fact published, it was not until about two weeks later,
July 19th, that Congress ordered the Declaration to
be engrossed and signed. This engrossing was not
completed until August 2d, and it was on that day
that most of the signatures were affixed to the parchment. At least fifteen of the signers were not in Philadelphia on that date, and their signatures were added
at various times during the months of August, September, October, and November. Thomas McKean,
from Delaware, usually said to be the last signer,
could have signed some time between August and
October, 1776, and Matthew Thornton, from New
Hampshire, signed in the latter part of 1776 or early
in 1777; but, with these possible exceptions, no signatures were added to the Declaration after the year,
immortal in American annals, of 1776.

II

DISCOVERY OF THE DECLARATION OF INDEPENDENCE BY THE PEOPLE OF THE UNITED STATES

IT seems incredible to us now that our Declaration of Independence remained for half a century a forgotten document to the American people and that Thomas Jefferson did not realize, until near the end of his life, that he had composed an epochal paper. Yet the evidence is solidly arrayed to this effect.

After the Declaration had played its part in our Revolutionary struggle, it slumbered in the archives of the Government until it was brought to popular attention by the enterprise of a writing teacher and a public controversy over the credit for the honor of its first popular publication, between this professor of penmanship and a rival publisher. To contend that the Declaration of Independence, one of the world's great documents of liberty, would have remained in unnoticed obscurity but for Benjamin Owen Tyler would be, of course, absurd. The rejuvenation of a healthy patriotism by the second war with Great Britain (the War of 1812), to which the final, blood-stirring victory at New Orleans contributed a sustaining energy, created a state of mind in the American people that made possible the commercial success of the publishing venture of the pen-artist, and that

Tyler was the first to popularize the Declaration by a widespread publication should not be forgotten.

The story of the writing of the Declaration, how it was composed, adopted, signed, and "submitted to a candid world," is too well known to justify recounting here; but a part of it may be retold for the sake of the continuity and completeness of this story.

On July 2, 1776, the Colonial delegates in the Continental Congress absolved, by vote, the United Colonies from all allegiance to the British Crown and, on July 4th, approved the draft of the form of announcement of this action. Thomas Jefferson's composition was the draft of this form of announcement and had been submitted to the Congress as the report of the Committee of Five, to whom had been entrusted the preparation of the document. As adopted by Congress, this report became the Declaration of Independence, and the last, rough draft of this report, in the handwriting of Jefferson and bearing certain changes in the handwriting of John Adams and Benjamin Franklin, was preserved among Jefferson's Papers. It was transferred, in this year of 1922, from the Department of State to the Library of Congress by order of the President of the United States.

This precious paper was immediately subjected to a searching and critical examination and all the physical facts respecting it noted down. In the course of this examination certain things heretofore unnoticed, became apparent. The most important of these is that Benjamin Franklin had more to do with the phraseology of the Declaration of Independence than has been recognized up to now. We will note these facts before proceeding with the story of the discovery of the Declaration by the people of the United States, as they are facts curiously interwoven with that discovery.

The rough draft of the Declaration, the report of the Committee of Five, because it bears pen changes by Adams and Franklin, is, presumably, the final rough draft from which Jefferson says he made a clean copy for submission to Congress. It bears numerous alterations, and, in the margins, opposite seven of these alterations, Jefferson has written the names of Adams and Franklin, each time with a little symbol, corresponding to a like symbol in the text as designating the word or words written in by these two men. But these marginal notes of identification by Jefferson *were written in many years after* 1776, and Jefferson's memory in this was as untrustworthy as it has been proven to be in many of his other recollections respecting the Declaration. He credits John Adams with two corrections and Benjamin Franklin with five. But Franklin should have been credited with *eleven* changes in all, and four of these, hitherto unnoted, are of the first importance.

In the very first line of this final, rough draft, Benjamin Franklin struck the resounding note that underlies our entire governmental theory and welded together Jefferson's rich phraseology as a hammer-stroke upon a deep-toned bell welds together all lesser notes in the vibrant air. For Jefferson had written: "When in the course of human events it becomes necessary for a people to dissolve the political bands," etc., and Benjamin Franklin crossed out the weak "a" and wrote "one," so that the line reads to all the world: "When in the course of human events it becomes necessary for one people," etc. And next, Jefferson, with too much doubt, perhaps, of what the Congress would really do, wrote: "they should declare the causes which impel them to threaten separation," and Franklin smashed out the hesitant "threaten" and wrote a firm "the" in its stead.

But the most ringing change of all comes in that well-known phrase: "We hold these truths to be," etc. Jefferson had written "sacred & undeniable"; but Franklin crossed them out and merits honor from every lover of liberty for his great substitution: "SELF-EVIDENT."

The next change is still of high importance. Jefferson wrote: "He has kept among us in times of peace standing armies & ships of war without our consent," and Franklin, ever watchful of the democracy he loved, changed this to: "without the consent of our Legislatures."

The next heretofore unnoted change was more a clarifying of idea than anything else, but still it was the clear genius of a master of language who could give his every word a polished value. Jefferson had written: "giving his assent to their pretended acts of legislation" and Franklin shifted this to read: "giving his assent to their acts of pretended legislation."

The last unnoted change was in that portion of Jefferson's draft which Congress expunged, so it is relatively immaterial; however, Jefferson wrote: "future ages will scarce believe that the hardiness of one man adventured, within the short compass of twelve years only" (and what follows of Jefferson's idea is so crossed over as to be indecipherable), but Franklin's change was "to lay a foundation so bold and undisguised for tyranny." Jefferson recorrected Franklin by crossing out the word "lay" and rewriting "build" in its stead, so that the finally corrected sentence read: "future ages will scarce believe that the hardiness of one man adventured, within the short space of twelve years only, to build a foundation so broad and undisguised for tyranny over a people fostered & fixed in principles of freedom."

How did Jefferson happen to remember five of Franklin's changes and not the other six? How was it that other important details of the composition and signing of that immortal paper could not be remembered by him? John Adams was equally forgetful. Thomas McKean, a signer, became quite confused in his remembrance, and the real facts, so far as obtainable, have been obtained by a critical study, analysis, and comparison of the documentary evidence that has survived.   Argument and discussion, recalling of events, attempts to remember, and a literature of controversy over the drafting and signing of the Declaration began, casually enough, in 1817, when Joseph Delaplaine, of Philadelphia, in writing a biographical sketch of Jefferson, asked him certain questions about the Declaration.   Jefferson's reply shows that even in 1817 he had not yet awakened to what he had accomplished, for he dismissed the matter briefly by saying that Adams and Franklin "each of them made two or three short and verbal alterations only, but even this is laying more stress on mere composition than it merits; for that alone was mine; the sentiments were of all America."

Two years later Samuel A. Welles asked Jefferson's aid in the preparation of a life of his grandfather, Samuel Adams, and Jefferson's letters to Welles, giving his recollections as to the Declaration, are much at variance with the established facts.   Why Jefferson did not recognize in 1776 the tremendous importance of his composition may, in a measure, be due to the severe criticism and rough treatment his effort received on the floor of Congress.   Jefferson says: "during the debate I was sitting near Dr. Franklin and he observed I was writhing a little under the acrimonious criticisms of some of its parts; and it was on that occasion that, by way of comfort, he told me the story of John Thompson, the Hatter, and his new sign." (Thompson had devised a new signboard for his hat shop, and his friends, one after another, criticised the various words thereon, and Thompson, following each bit of advice, struck out one word after another until nothing was left of the original composition except Thompson's name and the figure of a hat.) The severe treatment Jefferson's draft received seemed to have so injured his feelings that, after the Declaration was adopted, he put his draft away and did not refer to it or think about it again for nearly fifty years. That none of the other men of the Continental Congress of 1776 thought any more about it than did Jefferson is fairly plain from their inability, in after years, to remember very much about either the adoption or the signing. Like many other great things done by our Forefathers, the doing of them was the important thing, and, having done their best, they did not pause to emulate the classic example of Little Jack Horner on extracting the plum. The Declaration adopted, signed, and published to the world, was a thing done, for good or for evil, and the men of 1776 pressed on to the accomplishment of the heavy tasks still confronting them. That Jefferson, Adams, and others, competent to speak, could remember in after years very little about the matter is good evidence that the Declaration was viewed as a mere piece of routine work of small consequence, as compared with the vote of Independence of July 2d. Franklin died in 1790, before any of the later public interest had been displayed in the Declaration, which accounts for the fact that we have no story, or statement from him regarding it. John Adams placed all the emphasis upon the passage of the resolution of Independence on July 2d, and paid scant attention to the Declaration itself except to complain that the bells ringing far into the night of the celebration of July 8th kept him awake. With Jefferson it was much the same, so far as his attention to the Declaration was concerned. Any pride of authorship he may have had in his draft completely withered under the criticisms of the Congress. He would have gone to his grave without realizing what he had accomplished but for the attention drawn to the Declaration by a publisher's quarrel in 1818–19 and Timothy Pickering's Fourth of July oration in 1823.

As early as 1810 a Government clerk by the name of William P. Gardner, who was afterward United States Consul to Demerara, conceived the idea of publishing a decorative copy of the Declaration with facsimile signatures. He confided his plan and idea to an engraver and tentative sketches were made. In 1813 these tentative sketches were submitted to Jefferson for approval, and his comment thereon contains no word or hint of a realization of the place the Declaration was destined to occupy in the mind and heart of the world. The engraver, in whom Gardner confided, carried the entire scheme to John Binns, a publisher, in Philadelphia, and Binns, in 1816, advertised his intention of publishing the Declaration in a manner closely approximating Gardner's plan; but beyond this public announcement he seems to have done nothing.

Benjamin Owen Tyler removed from New York City to Washington, in 1817, and then saw, for the first time, the Declaration of Independence. Being a professional penman and an instructor of writing, he was ever on the lookout for material of a striking character with which to display his skill. He asked for and obtained permission to copy the Declaration and make facsimiles of the signatures. This copy he made, exactly the size of the original. The text he engrossed and enlarged, and ornamented the important words, so that while not a facsimile it was a most perfect and beautiful specimen of ornamental lettering and pen skill. The signatures he copied in exact facsimile. Acting Secretary of State, Richard Rush, certified September 10, 1817, that the text was correctly copied and that he had "examined the signatures to each. Those executed by Mr. Tyler are curiously exact imitations; so much so that it would be difficult if not impossible for the closest scrutiny to distinguish them, were it not for the hand of time, from the originals."

This copy Tyler had engraved and published in 1818, and Binns, who had been taking his time with the Gardner idea, found himself forestalled. He immediately published an attack upon Tyler and upon Tyler's publication. Gardner joined forces with Tyler and a publisher's war ensued in the public prints.

Despite his best efforts, Binns did not succeed in getting his Declaration on the market until the next year. It was on the same plan as to decorated text and facsimile signatures as Tyler's, but where Tyler displayed nothing but the text and signatures, Binns enclosed the Declaration in an elaborate ornamental chain made up of the seals of the Thirteen original States, surmounted by portraits of Washington, Hancock, and Jefferson, which Tyler naïvely remarked, "do not ornament the original any more than plates did the Bible when first given to man." Binns's seals were drawn by Thomas Sully and his portraits were from paintings by Stuart, Otis, and Copley. John Quincy Adams, then Secretary of State, certified to the correctness of the copy of the text and facsimiles of the signatures.

Tyler's publication of the Declaration had met with great success; Binns's also was not slow in selling, and the advertising they both received from their controversy in print aroused interest in the Declaration as a document regardless of its effect upon the fortunes of the rival publishers. This interest steadily increased, and in 1823 Timothy Pickering delivered a Fourth of July oration at Salem, Massachusetts, in which, on the authority of John Adams, he made several statements regarding the Declaration to which Jefferson took exception and aired these exceptions in a long and caustic letter to James Madison, giving the facts according to his, Jefferson's, recollection:

Mr. Adams's memory has led him into unquestionable error; at the age of eighty-eight, and forty-seven years after the transactions of Independence, this is not wonderful, nor should I, at the age of eighty, on the small advantage of that difference only, venture to oppose my memory to his, were it not supported by written notes, taken by myself, at the moment and on the spot. . . . You have seen the original paper, now in my hands, with the corrections of Dr. Franklin and Mr. Adams interlined in their own handwritings. Their alterations were two or three only and merely verbal.

These "notes taken . . . at the moment and on the spot" have survived, but they do not add anything to what has been gleaned from a critical analysis of all the other available sources, for they merely state, in less than thirty words, that Jefferson drafted the Declaration and reported it to Congress. The fact of the matter is that when Jefferson, half a century after the event, found the Declaration assuming an importance he had never dreamed it would, he was unwilling, apparently, to admit that its composition was thought of such minor consequence in 1776 that he had then failed to note the facts respecting its creation, and, in 1823, was also unwilling to admit that he could not fully recall them.

It must have been after 1819 and probably it was at the time of the 1823 controversy that Jefferson looked through his papers for the draft of the Declaration and made the marginal notes thereon of the Franklin and Adams changes. At that late day, forty-seven years afterwards, Jefferson's failure to recognize all of

Franklin's changes becomes measurably explainable. That these marginal notes were not made until many years after 1776 is clear from the fact that the draft, folded and filed away among Jefferson's papers, had broken in one of the folds from age. To remedy this, Jefferson pasted a narrow strip of paper vertically down the outer margin of the first page to repair the break. There can be no other reason than this for pasting this strip at such a place, as there is no writing under it, and, after pasting this bit of paper in place, Jefferson wrote two of his marginal notes *across* it. This condition effectually militates against any theory that the marginal notes, identifying the Adams and Franklin handwritings, were made in 1776.

Had it not been for the patriotism aroused by the successful War of 1812, the enterprise and artistic skill of Benjamin Owen Tyler in 1817, and Timothy Pickering's oration in 1823, with the ensuing public controversies from the last two happenings, it is quite possible that John Quincy Adams, while Secretary of State, might not have thought it worth while to have an exact and official facsimile made of the entire Declaration of Independence, signatures and all. This he did in 1823, and this facsimile is the only complete and exact facsimile that has ever been made from the original Declaration. Every other facsimile has been made from one of these 1823 facsimiles or its replica. The original plate of the 1823 reproduction is still in the custody of the Department of State.

There seems to be no documentary evidence available regarding the exact process by which this 1823 facsimile was made. Among the methods of reproductive copper-plate engraving then known in the United States was a wet sheet transfer from the original to be engraved. Because of this there exists a tradition that the ink upon the parchment was then loosened and that the Declaration has been fading ever since, until now it is barely legible. This has not yet been proved, however, and so many other factors enter into the matter that it is not at all a conclusive explanation of the present physical condition of the parchment. Richard Rush's statement as to "the hand of time" in his certificate to Tyler's facsimile signatures furnishes food for thought as to the condition of the signatures in 1817.

As to the physical condition of the Declaration at the present time, in this year of 1924, it may be said that, while greatly faded, it has faded almost uniformly, and the text, while difficult to read, is still fairly legible. Under certain angles of light it is perfectly so. It is the signatures that have suffered the most, and, while the greater number of these have almost disappeared, every one of them can still be made out with the aid of a good reading-glass. It is quite doubtful if all trace of any of them will ever completely vanish, and, until documentary or other strong evidence is produced, it is not quite reasonable to put the blame for the present condition of the Declaration upon the shoulders of the engraver of 1823, who was one of the best of the few copper-plate engravers then in America.

Congress immediately assumed charge of John Quincy Adams's facsimile and, by a resolution of May 26, 1824, directed a very thorough distribution, over the entire country, of a total edition of two hundred copies. Two copies each were to be given to the surviving signers (the two sent to Jefferson were on parchment), to the President of the United States, the Vice President, to James Madison, and to the Marquis de Lafayette; twenty copies were allotted to Congress, twelve to the Government Departments, two to the President's house, two to the Supreme Court room, one to the Governor of each State, one to each branch of each State legislature, one to the Governor of each Territory, one to the legislative council of each Territory, and the remainder to different universities and colleges as the President of the United States might direct. This judiciously planned distribution which placed a perfect reproduction of the Declaration in the principal centers of the entire country completed, in a masterly and official manner, the work begun as a private venture by Benjamin Owen Tyler half a dozen years before.

The Centennial Exposition in Philadelphia, at which the original Declaration was exhibited, inspired another wave of reproduction by private publishers, and since 1876 our charter of American liberty has been reproduced oftener in facsimile and print than any other known document. Some of these reproductions are fearful and wonderful examples of design and supposedly decorative embellishment which tax the possibilities of the printer's art to the limit. The reproduction of the Declaration in type has not been confined entirely to America; its appeal has ceased to be to America alone, for its clarion note of liberty finds a responsive echo in every corner of the world to-day.

The Declaration of Independence was composed for the single purpose of justifying to the world the breaking away of the Colonies from Great Britain. It was designed to introduce, in the most persuasive and convincing form, the right and justice of the adoption of Richard Henry Lee's resolution of Independence. It was a campaign document in world politics, though much was hoped for, from its argumentative strength, in the Colonies themselves, for it drew the line sharply between Patriot and Tory and forced every one to take sides plainly for or against Great Britain. It was intended to put an end to vacillation and to make the Colonial cause a clean-cut issue. How well Jefferson performed this task and fulfilled these intentions the world has judged, and no amount of intensive study and critical comparison of historical fact can ever take from him his rightful glory of being the herald of American liberty.

III

THE TRAVELS OF THE DECLARATION OF INDEPENDENCE

For one hundred years after the Declaration of Independence had been given to the world, that immortal document was without a permanent home. It moved through ten different cities and towns, scattered hither and yon through five different States. Three times it was hurriedly carried off to escape capture, or destruction, at the hands of the troopers of the king of the country against whom its thunder was and had been directed, and once, at least, its transfer to other quarters saved it from flames that completely gutted the supposedly fireproof Government building in which it had been stored. In its wanderings it has rested for periods ranging from a few hours to several years, and the longest times it has been in any one place have been thirty-six and forty-four years, respectively. Both of these lengthy periods were spent in Washington, D.C., the first in the United States Patent Office and the second in the present building of the Department of State. The cities and towns which have had the honor of harboring the Declaration are: Philadelphia, Lancaster, and York, Pennsylvania; Trenton and Princeton, New Jersey; New York City;

Annapolis and Baltimore, Maryland; Leesburg, Virginia, and Washington, D.C.

The Declaration has been out of the Government's hands but twice since 1776; once by force of circumstances and once by favor. It did not possess a real, permanent home for one hundred and one years after its birth, and this home was the huge granite building in the Capital of the Nation, just west of the White House which is known to Washingtonians as the State, War and Navy Building. In the library of the Department of State section of this structure the Declaration remained undisturbed for a longer period of time than it had ever before experienced. From here it went upon what will probably be its last journey when it was transferred in 1921 to the Library of Congress by special order of the President of the United States.

The travels of the Declaration since July, 1776, are interesting in many ways; they are typical of the early, unsettled state of our democratic experiment in government, and the latter portion of those wanderings exemplify a mistaken idea in government economy in not making proper provision for preserving the important records of our past.

The first journey of the Declaration was from Philadelphia to Baltimore, in the same year that saw the signing of that historical parchment. After the Declaration was engrossed and signed, it was filed in the office of Charles Thomson, the Secretary of the Con-

tinental Congress, whose office was in the building
where the Congress sat, the Pennsylvania State
House, later to be known as Independence Hall. Like
all parchment documents it was rolled up (there is no
indication that the Declaration was ever folded) and
rested undisturbed in Thomson's file, except when
brought out to be signed by different delegates, until
the near approach of the British, closely pursuing
Washington, forced the Commander-in-Chief across
the Delaware River. Congress hastily adjourned
from Philadelphia, December 12th, to reconvene in
Baltimore, eight days later. The papers and records,
including the Declaration, were packed into two light
wagons, which Congress had purchased for its own use
in October, and carried to the Maryland city. It was
here that the Declaration was published, in printed
form, for the second time, by order of Congress, and,
in this publication, the names of the signers were
made public for the first time. Washington's brilliant
victories at Trenton and Princeton forced the British
out of West Jersey, and early in March, 1777, Congress returned to Philadelphia. After a short visit of a
little over two months the Declaration returned to its
first home. In September, 1777, came another alarm.
This time the British moved by water to the head of
Chesapeake Bay, to march overland against Philadelphia from the south. Brandywine, where Washington
shook the British confidence; Red Bank, where the
Hessians under Count Donop suffered a bloody re-

pulse; Fort Island, in the Delaware, that withstood terrific bombardment and destroyed two fine British ships, and Washington's excellent maneuvering held Howe in check for a time; but the end was inevitable. Congress adjourned to Lancaster, Pennsylvania, when it became apparent that Philadelphia could not be saved. It was offered quarters in the court-house where the Pennsylvania Legislature was then sitting; this was not to its taste so it removed to York. The Declaration of Independence remained in the York court-house until the news came that the British had evacuated Philadelphia. The papers and records were again packed in wagons and jolted down the old York road into Philadelphia. July 2, 1778, the Declaration was home once more in Philadelphia.

In the year 1777, the first anniversary of the Declaration passed unnoticed. The situation then was depressing. Burgoyne was advancing from Canada and Schuyler was retreating before him; Howe had sailed from New York and the entire coast from Massachusetts to the Carolinas was in dread; Congress was distraught with the difficulties that pressed in upon all sides. But in June, 1778, matters had improved greatly. Lafayette and De Kalb had come and France had definitely promised aid; the British had fled from Philadelphia and been severely mauled in their retreat across Jersey; confidence had replaced doubt. Congress ordered July 4th to be celebrated as a holiday, and our annual national celebrations date from this year of 1778. The army, then at Brunswick Landing, fired a salute of thirteen guns, the troops paraded and fired a musketry *feu de joie*, a running discharge along the entire front, and gave three cheers for the "Perpetual and Undisturbed Independence of the United States of America." The men adorned their hats with "green boughs," and a double allowance of rum was served in honor of the day.

The Declaration remained in the State House, Philadelphia, from July, 1778, to June, 1783, when the mutinous conduct of soldiers of the Pennsylvania Line brought about an adjournment to Princeton, New Jersey. This move again started the Declaration on its wanderings for, once away from Philadelphia, it seemed easy for Congress to change to a new location, and each of the next two succeeding years saw it in a new place. At Annapolis, in Maryland, in November, 1783; in Trenton, New Jersey, a year later, and in New York City in June, 1785. Here it stayed until the Continental Congress faded out of existence to be replaced by a Congress of the United States under the new Constitution in 1789.

In New York, the Declaration and the Congress occupied the second story of the old City Hall building, then at the northeast corner of Wall and Nassau Streets. When the first Congress under the Constitution convened, the venerable Charles Thomson formally turned over to President George Washington all the papers and records of the Continental Congress,

FEDERAL HALL IN WALL STREET, NEW YORK

Where the Declaration of Independence was kept from 1785 to 1789

including, of course, the Declaration. These papers were given into the custody of the newly created Department of State, and so remained in New York until December, 1790, when Congress met in Philadelphia. Once again the Declaration was in the city of its birth; but this time it was not deposited in Independence Hall, but in the various buildings which were occupied by the United States Department of State; first on Market Street, at Arch and Sixth, and next at Fifth and Chestnut.

In 1800, the transfer of the Capital of the United States was made to its agreed upon permanent site, the District of Columbia, and when the records and papers reached the Potomac the only building far enough advanced to offer them protection was the one intended for the use of the Treasury; in this the Secretary of State, his office and records were forced to take shelter. After two months of this crowded hospitality the Department of State and its archives moved to Nineteenth and Pennsylvania Avenue, into a group of structures, then just finished and called the "Seven Buildings." Less than a year later the Declaration and other papers were transferred to the old War Office Building, then on Seventeenth Street, where the west front of the present State, War and Navy Building now stands. Here the Declaration remained undisturbed until the War of 1812 again involved it in sudden and precipitate movement which started another period of traveling that did not end for over sixty years.

In August, 1814, a British expedition sailed up the Chesapeake Bay and marched overland from the Patuxent against Washington. After a skirmish at Bladensburg, the British troops entered the city, and, with wanton torch, gave the Government buildings to the flames. The official report of the British officer in command stated that his troops were fired upon from the houses and the Capitol building itself; but no citizen nor soldier was captured as a result, and none were court-martialed or executed for such indefensible conduct; with exemplary military restraint the Capitol and other Government buildings were burned only in retaliation.

To the good judgment of Secretary of State, James Monroe, and the activity and energy of three Department of State employees, Chief Clerk John Graham, Josiah King, and Stephen Pleasanton, we are indebted for the saving of the Declaration of Independence, the Constitution of the United States, and other priceless records of our country. Monroe sent orders from Benedict, Maryland, whither he had gone to reconnoiter the British movement, to pack and remove the records of the Department at once. Bags had already been prepared and the three clerks set to work with a will. Into these coarse linen sacks all the papers of the Department were packed. The Declaration, the Constitution, Washington's commission as Commander-in-Chief, and treaties between the United States and foreign powers, among them treaties with the very nation from whose soldiers those selfsame treaties had to be protected. The work done by these three Government clerks was thorough and complete. Some volumes of the early printed laws and miscellaneous correspondence had to be left behind, and were destroyed by the British, but Secretary Monroe's report, after the war, stated the belief that all the papers and records of the old Congress and those of the Department itself, except the above-mentioned laws and papers, were saved.

There was considerable difficulty in obtaining wagons, but a sufficient number were finally secured and Pleasanton traveled with them. They left the city by way of old Georgetown, and crossed into Virginia by way of the Chain Bridge. Pleasanton stored the records in Edgar Patterson's barn, about two miles above Chain Bridge; but, the next day, fearing the British might send a raiding party to destroy a cannon foundry near by, he obtained new teams from the country folk and made a long and dusty trip of about thirty-five miles to Leesburg. Here he stored the papers in the house of the Reverend Mr. Littlejohn, locked them up securely, and turned into bed a completely exhausted man. That night the British put Washington to the flames, and the next day Pleasanton learned that many of the Leesburg folk had seen a dull, angry glow in the east that told of the burning of the Capital.

But the Declaration was safe. Pleasanton returned

to Washington two days later to find the President's house and other buildings still smouldering. The papers he had saved were not brought back to the city for some weeks, when all danger of the return of the British had disappeared. When the Declaration and the other papers were brought back from Leesburg, they were placed in a building on the south side of G Street, near Eighteenth, until the destruction wrought by the British could be repaired. In 1820, the Department of State moved into a Government building, then erected on the site of the present Treasury Department.

In 1841, the white marble Patent Office, still standing at Seventh and F Streets, was finished. Substantial in appearance and built with the best of care, as care in building was then understood, it was supposed to be fireproof and, as the Patent Office was then under the control and was a bureau of the Department of State, the valuable and interesting historical papers and relics were transferred to it and placed on exhibition in its Hall of Models. The Declaration of Independence and Washington's commission as Commander-in-Chief were among the things sent, and these two parchments were placed in a single frame and hung up to public view. For thirty-five years these two precious American documents hung exposed to the light, and it was this long exposure, unprotected in any way from chill of winter and the glare and heat of summer, that has caused both the Declaration and the Commission to fade out to a uniform dimness. But it is some consolation to know that, while the Declaration has faded greatly, the entire text is still legible; it is the signatures that have suffered the most, and these from other causes than exposure to light alone.

From 1842 to 1876, the Declaration of Independence slowly faded in the Patent Office exhibition hall, and it might have continued there until the damage became total had not the Centennial year of 1876 stirred up a new interest in matters historical. In that year a great exposition was planned in Philadelphia, the first of the great national and international expositions that have been held in the United States since then. The managers of this exposition applied for the loan of the Declaration as a feature of the centennial celebration. They wished to display it in Independence Hall, as a more fitting place than in the grounds of the exposition itself, and they had prepared a special, fireproof safe, with a heavy glass door, behind which the parchment could be viewed. They offered to lock this door, turn the key over to the Government, and let the Department of State seal the lock. The Government had, however, already decided to send the Declaration to Philadelphia as a part of its own exhibit in the United States building there, but the exposition managers wanted it in Independence Hall. After some argument in which the Philadelphians used George W. Childs as an influence, President Grant directed that the Declaration be deposited in Independence Hall. The parchment was taken to Philadelphia by Alonzo Bell, chief clerk of the Patent Office, and the newspaper notices of the day noted the fact that the Declaration had greatly faded..

Secretary of State Richard Rush is on record as noting, as early as the year 1817, that the signatures then showed the effects of time, so that the reasons for the present condition of the Declaration, both as to text and signatures, must be sought in more than one place and in more than one period. The Declaration, evidently, was subjected to careless or improper handling for years prior to 1841. Until it was framed by the Patent Office for exhibition purposes it had been kept rolled up, a method of storing parchments that has been used from time immemorial. It had been rolled and unrolled hundreds of times, and the many creases and cracks in the surface of the parchment, caused by this rolling being done carelessly, is the reason for the damage to the signatures. The text of the Declaration was engrossed by a professional penman, a man who was careful of the quality of his ink, and the rolling and unrolling of the parchment has not affected his work, except in the large lettered heading, where the ink was laid on extra thick. Ink does not bite into parchment as it does into paper; it lies more on the surface, dries on the surface and scales off more readily than it does when laid on paper. The large printed heading of the Declaration shows this scaling off in the same manner, but not to such a pitiful extent as do the signatures. The curl of the parchment shows that it was the custom to roll it up with the writing on the inside, and its condition indicates that the rolling commenced at the top of the Declaration; the signatures of the Signers, therefore, were the first and the last to be handled in unrolling and rolling up the parchment. They received the maximum amount of rubbing. The ink with which the signatures were written varied in quality. The Declaration was not signed by all the delegates on the same day; there was, consequently, different ink used during the period of time in which the signing was done — the record shows that this signing stretched over a period of several months. Ink, in Revolutionary times, was made from a powder; the bottled liquid known to us was unknown to our Revolutionary Fathers, who mixed their own writing fluid by adding water to this prepared powder. None of the ink, thus made on different days, appeared to have the biting quality of the carefully prepared ink in which the text of the Declaration was engrossed. The signatures were thus more easily scaled off, and they did scale off, more than they faded, while the text itself merely faded out in an almost uniform degree. Nowhere in the text does the writing show the slightest evidence of scaling; the only place where such an effect is discernible is in the large decorative letters in the caption heading, where the ink, as before stated, was laid on extra thick. The worst creases and cracks in the parchment run vertically through the three middle columns of signatures, and the signatures in these particular columns are the ones that have suffered the most damage.

The comment aroused by the appearance of the Declaration in 1876, resulted in the passage of a joint resolution of Congress, directing the Secretary of the Interior, the Secretary of the Smithsonian Institution, and the Librarian of Congress to take steps to restore the Declaration, a typical example of governmental method in caring for its priceless records; the horse had been stolen, so the stable door was to be officially locked; but it was not until four years later that the door was even closed. In 1880, the Secretary of the Interior called this committee together, and the conclusion reached was to summon a committee of the American Academy of Science to look into the matter. This Academy committee reported that "press copies had been taken from the original so that part of the ink had been removed from the parchment," thus continuing the questionable tradition for which not the slightest evidence now seems to be available. Fortunately, it was decided best to make no attempt to restore the Declaration, and all that the Government can do from now on is to hold the parchment in the exact condition it is at present. All of the present legibility of the parchment can be held and sustained, and further fading can be almost entirely prevented, or at least held against every enemy except time itself.

The exhibition of the Declaration at Philadelphia in 1876, in Independence Hall, which was a long distance from the exposition grounds, probably inspired several publishers and business firms to issue facsimiles that could be distributed, or disposed of in the grounds themselves. The exact degree of influence exercised by this cannot be shown, of course, but, at any rate, a wave of patriotism swept over the country at the time of the Centennial, and on the crest of it came a flood of facsimiles. Since then the output of replicas of the Declaration has been so consistently steady that it now has been reproduced a greater number of times than any other document of American history.

When the exposition was over, the citizens of Philadelphia tried to obtain permission to hold the Declaration permanently in Independence Hall, but the Government was not acquiescent. Philadelphia did manage to retain possession for a short time. But finally the Department of State requisitioned the Department of the Interior, under which the Patent Office then functioned, and the Department of the Interior requested the return of the Declaration from Independence Hall, and the Declaration was returned through precisely this same process, only reversed.

Along with the Declaration, the Interior Department returned Washington's commission, Franklin's cane, Washington's camp chest, and all the other

relics that had been in the custody of the Patent
Office. This was in March, 1877, and this transfer
probably saved the Declaration and these other memorials from destruction, for, a few months later, the
supposedly fireproof Patent Office caught fire and two
wings of the building were completely gutted before
the flames could be controlled.

The Declaration, when received by the Department of State from the Interior Department, was
placed on exhibition in the Library of the present
building (the State, War and Navy Building), which
had then just been completed, and here it remained
for nearly a score of years, until its condition appeared
to have become so desperate that it was withdrawn
from public view. About 1894 it was placed, along
with the Constitution, in a specially constructed steel
safe, in the library of the Department, and was not
shown thereafter except on special order of the Secretary of State himself.

In 1921, twenty-seven years later, both Declaration
and Constitution were removed from this safe by
order of the President of the United States and transferred to the Library of Congress for their better preservation and exhibition to the public under proper
safeguards. This last removal of the Declaration had
nothing of glamour or romance about it; but was accomplished with fitting democratic simplicity. The
Secretary of State and the Librarian of Congress were
present when the safe containing the Declaration and

the Constitution was opened; both documents were carried by Library of Congress employees to the Library's mail wagon, and, resting upon a pile of leather United States mail sacks for a cushion, guarded by three young Americans who were fully conscious of the unexpected honor that had fallen to their lot, the Declaration whirled down the rain-washed asphalt of Pennsylvania Avenue, unnoticed and unheeded amid the crowded traffic of a September afternoon, to the gold-domed, granite Library building, in front of the United States Capitol. Here, along with the Constitution, in a special marble and bronze shrine, under artificial light, in which the damage causing actinic ray has been carefully neutralized, these charters of American liberty and government are displayed to the public. Under the plans worked out no further fading from this exposure is possible, and this exhibition was installed at the direction of the President of the United States "to satisfy," as President Harding has fittingly expressed it, "the laudable wish of patriotic Americans to have an opportunity to see the original fundamental documents upon which rest their independence and their Government."

IV

WASHINGTON'S HEADQUARTERS IN SEVEN STATES

THE line of march of the main Continental Army during the long eight years of hardship and battle of the Revolutionary War marks out the road our ancestors traveled to reach the haven of national independence, and Washington's Headquarters are the mile-stones by which we trace that road upon the page of history.

All of our Revolutionary sentiment clusters around these spots. From William Keith's farmhouse from whence issued the orders for the desperate dash on Trenton; from the camp at Schuylkill Falls from whence came the manly thanks to the defeated troops of Brandywine; from the sober announcement, in the fields before Yorktown, of the surrender of Cornwallis, to the farewell orders to the armies from Rocky Hill, every spot is a landmark in the struggle for righteous control of our destinies and freedom for our native land. It is regrettable that so many of the buildings used as Headquarters have disappeared through neglect and inattention of early days, but those that remain have been properly marked and are now being carefully preserved.

But seven States can claim the distinction of having had Headquarters of the Continental Army within their borders. These are: Massachusetts, New York,

WASHINGTON'S HEADQUARTERS AT NEWBURGH, N.Y.

New Jersey, Pennsylvania, Delaware, Maryland, and
Virginia. New Jersey possesses the greatest number
of these headquarters locations, with New York and
Pennsylvania next. The movements of the main Continental Army were, of course, the backbone movements of the entire struggle, and, while the northern
and southern campaigns were of inestimable value in
deciding the issue, it is to the main army under Washington that we must look for a clear understanding of
the military history of the Revolution. It is curious to
follow the geographic shifting of the scene of action
and to note how the tide of war rose from the extreme
eastern boundary of the colonies to sweep like a flood
down the entire coast length and inland until it beat
upon the Appalachian barrier. After Boston the fighting swept westward to New York, New Jersey, and
Pennsylvania. To and fro across these three States it
moiled and roiled for five of the eight years of the war;
then its wave swept onward to Virginia, the geo-
graphical center of the colonies, faltered, broke upon
the ramparts of Yorktown, ebbed back to New York,
and within that harbor its eddies subsided to the
calms of peace.

Throughout the eight years of war the path of the
struggle may best be followed by the date lines of the
series of general orders issued by Washington, the
locations of whose Headquarters may be established
by these orders and the accounts and vouchers of his
expenses as Commander-in-Chief. Except where the

State authorities directed that certain quarters be placed at his disposal, or where Tory property was commandeered, the Commander-in-Chief paid for the use of every house he occupied as Headquarters throughout the entire war.

The first Headquarters of the conflict was in the Wadsworth house at Cambridge, built by Harvard College in 1726, for the use of its presidents, generally known as the "President's House," and at that time occupied by President Samuel Langdon. Near the middle of July the house of John Vassall, then a fugitive Loyalist, was prepared for Washington's occupancy. The Twenty-First Massachusetts Regiment, commanded by Colonel John Glover, and known as the Marblehead Regiment, had been quartered in the house, and after its removal it took eight days' cleaning to render it habitable. The house is now known as the Craigie-Longfellow house, from its owners, Dr. Andrew Craigie and Henry Wadsworth Longfellow, six of whose children were born under its roof. Jared Sparks and Edward Everett were among those who occupied this house at various times. The Headquarters remained here until Washington left Cambridge.

After the evacuation of Boston, the British fleet and troop-ships lay in the lower harbor, out of range of cannon shot, for ten days. When they finally sailed, their destination could only be conjectural. It was assumed to be New York City, and Washington left

Cambridge April 4, 1776, for that place. On his arrival, Headquarters were established in a house on
Pearl Street. After the Commander-in-Chief returned
from Philadelphia, whither he had been summoned by
Congress, Headquarters were established, June 7th,
in the Motier house which stood at what is now the
corner of Varick and Charlton Streets. After the retreat from Long Island and the decision to abandon
New York, Washington's quarters were at Robert
Murray's house, near Thirty-Second Street and
Fourth Avenue. September 15th he was at Mott's
Tavern, Harlem Plains. The British forced a landing
on this date, on Manhattan Island at Kip's Bay, at
what is now about the foot of Thirty-Fourth Street,
and the inexplicable panic of the American troops on
this occasion has furnished us a record of one of the
rare instances of rage overbalancing Washington's
usual calm judgment. After the battle of Harlem
Heights, Headquarters were established at the Roger
Morris house, now better known as the Jumel man-
sion; it had been erected by Colonel Roger Morris
who married a daughter of Frederick Phillipse, owner
of Phillipse Manor, which covered the larger part of
Westchester, Dutchess, and Putnam Counties, New
York.

For over a month the American and British troops
faced each other until a flanking movement by the
latter forced the Continentals to fall back to White
Plains. Headquarters were at Valentine's Hill Octo-

ber 21st and 22d, and on the 23d at the Miller house at White Plains. After the battle at the Plains, October 28th, and the unexpected move of the British ten days later, the Commander-in-Chief made a rapid tour of inspection of the defenses of the Hudson as far up as West Point and then shifted the army to the west side of the river. Headquarters were at Hackensack, New Jersey, November 15th, at the house of Peter Zabriskie. The British stormed and captured Fort Washington, November 16th, and four days later crossed the Hudson and advanced in force upon Fort Lee. Weakened by the loss of the men surrendered at Fort Washington and the criminal delay of Major-General Charles Lee in reinforcing him, Washington withdrew the troops from the fort to prevent a repetition of the Fort Washington disaster, and the retreat through the Jerseys began. The general orders for November 10, 1776, to January 12, 1777, which cover this movement and the Trenton-Princeton campaign, have been missing since before the year 1780, so that the Headquarters locations for this interesting period and until the army reached Morristown after the battle of Princeton have been established from other sources. It should be remembered that not every place where the Commander-in-Chief passed the day or night was, in fact, Headquarters; properly speaking, only those places from which general orders were issued should be considered as the Headquarters of the Continental Army. Of these one hundred and eighteen or so locations, eight are best known, and of these eight, seven were winter quarters, the exception being Fredericksburg, now in Putnam County, New York. The seven are: Cambridge, Massachusetts; Morristown and Middlebrook, New Jersey; Valley Forge, Pennsylvania; New Windsor, West Point (Moore's house), and Newburgh, New York.

The retreat through the Jerseys began November 21, 1776, and on December 8th Washington crossed the Delaware at Trenton and removed all the water craft to the west bank. Lack of means for crossing held the British, and the Headquarters, until the second advance into Jersey, after the Trenton victory, were at Thomas Barclay's "Summer Seat" at Morrisville, in Bucks County, Pennsylvania, opposite Trenton; at William Keith's farmhouse on the Brownsburg road near the upper fords of the Delaware; at Newtown, in the house of John Harris, and at Trenton, December 30th, in the house of the Loyalist, Major John Barnes, on Green Street. After the dash through the British lines and the victory at Princeton, the army reached Morristown, January 6, 1777, and went into winter quarters. Headquarters were at Jacob Arnold's tavern, which was a frame building and is not now standing. Here they remained until May 28th when the Commander-in-Chief moved to Middlebrook, which is now the same as Bound Brook, and there remained through the month of June. A period of uncertainty followed; the British plans were obscure and their object difficult to judge. Preparations for an expedition were made in New York, and the Continental Army moved slowly back and forth as the spy reports seemed to show that the Hudson Highlands or Philadelphia was in view. The fleet that sailed from New York finally entered Chesapeake Bay and the Continentals hurried into a position between the head of that bay and Philadelphia. Washington's Headquarters during these weeks of uncertainty were at Quibbletown, Middlebrook, Morristown, Pompton Plains, Van Aulen's, Smith's Clove, New York, and Galloway's in the Clove, which is within easy reach of the Highlands; then, as the news came that the expedition had really sailed from Sandy Hook, the army started on its rapid march to protect Philadelphia. The Headquarters on this march were again at Ramapo, New Jersey, Pompton, Morristown, Coryell's Ferry, Colonel Henry Hill's at Roxboro, Pennsylvania, at Cross Roads (Neshaminy Camp), Stanton, Darby, Wilmington, Delaware, Newport, and Birmingham. The battle of the Brandywine was fought September 11th, and the army retreated by way of Germantown and Chester and skirmished again with the advancing British at Yellow Springs, Pennsylvania, September 16th. From there on the locations of the Headquarters show Washington's efforts to protect Philadelphia by clever maneuvering; the general orders are dated from Reading Furnace, Potts Grove, Pennypacker's Mills,

Skippack, and Peter Wentz's in Worcester township. On October 4th Washington again risked an action at Germantown in the defense of Philadelphia. The next day Headquarters were at Perkiomen; next at Towamencin, in the house of Frederick Wampole, which is no longer standing; October 16th they were again at Peter Wentz's; October 20th, at James Morris's in Whitpain township, which house is now known as "Dawesfield" from Abraham Dawes, father of Mrs. Morris, who built it in 1736. November 2d, at Whitemarsh, Headquarters were in the house of George Emlen; both "Dawesfield" and Emlen's are still standing, but have been considerably altered in appearance by repairs and additions. At Emlen's, Headquarters remained for over a month, and on December 11th the army started on its march to winter quarters to the spot that has become synonymous with suffering in our Revolutionary annals — Valley Forge.

In Washington's letters very few comments upon his quarters are to be found, and even at Valley Forge, where every possible hardship of body and worry of mind was experienced, his feeling was for the suffering troops under his command, and no word of complaint for his own physical inconveniences. From his canvas tent on a freezing hillside came the well-known letter of protest at the criticisms leveled at his management of the army, and the restrained bitterness of its phrases furnish us with a picture of the inroads the suffering of the troops had made upon the Commander-in-Chief's iron self-control. He himself did not move under a roof at Valley Forge until the log huts were finished and his troops were able to abandon their tents. Two days before Christmas he wrote to the President of Congress:

Unless some great and capital change suddenly takes place . . . this army must inevitably be reduced to one or other of these three things: starve, dissolve, or disperse in order to obtain subsistence in the best manner they can. Rest assured, Sir, this is not an exaggerated picture, and that I have abundant reason to suppose what I say . . . three or four days of bad weather would prove our destruction. What then is to become of the army this winter? And if we are so often without provisions now, what is to become of us in the spring, when our force will be collected, with the aid perhaps of militia to take advantage of an early campaign, before the enemy can be reinforced? These are considerations of great magnitude, meriting the closest attention; and they will, when my own reputation is so intimately connected with the event and to be affected by it, justify my saying, that the present commissaries are by no means equal to the execution of the office, . . . though I have been tender heretofore of giving my opinion, or lodging complaints, as the change in that department took place contrary to my judgment and the consequences thereof were predicted; yet, finding that the inactivity of the army, whether for want of provisions, clothes, or other essentials, is charged to my account, not only by the common vulgar but by those in power, it is time to speak plain in exculpation of myself . . . the inability of an army, under the circumstances of this, to perform the common duties of soldiers (besides a number of men confined to hospitals for want of shoes, and others in farmhouses on the same

account), we have, by a field return this day made, no less
than two thousand, eight hundred and ninety-eight men
now in camp unfit for duty, because they are barefoot and
otherwise naked . . . our numbers fit for duty, from the
hardships and exposures they have undergone, particularly
on account of blankets (numbers having been obliged, and
still are, to sit up all night by fires, instead of taking comfortable rest in a natural and common way), have de-
creased near two thousand men.

We find gentlemen, without knowing whether the army
was really going into winter-quarters or not (for I am sure
no resolution of mine would warrant the Remonstrance),
reprobating the measure as much as if they thought the
soldiers were made of stocks or stones, and equally insen-
sible of frost and snow; and moreover, as if they conceived
it easily practicable for an inferior army, under the disad-
vantages I have described ours to be which are by no
means exaggerated, to confine a superior one, in all respects
well appointed and provided for a winter's campaign,
within the city of Philadelphia, and to cover from depreda-
tion and waste the states of Pennsylvania and Jersey. But
what makes this matter still more extraordinary in my eye
is, that these very gentlemen, — who were well apprized of
the nakedness of the troops from ocular demonstration,
who thought their own soldiers worse clad than others, and
who advised me near a month ago to postpone the execution of a plan I was about to adopt, in consequence of a
resolve for seizing clothes, under strong assurances that an
ample supply would be collected in ten days agreeably to a
decree of the State (not one article of which, by the by, is
yet come to hand), — should think a winter's campaign,
and the covering of these States from the invasion of an
enemy, so easy and practicable a business. I can assure
these gentlemen, that it is a much easier and less distress-
ing thing to draw remonstrances in a comfortable room by
a good fireside, than to occupy a cold, bleak hill, and sleep

under frost and snow, without clothes or blankets. However, although they seem to have little feeling for the naked and distressed soldiers, I feel superabundantly for them, and, from my soul, I pity those miseries, which it is neither in my power to relieve or prevent. . . . I am obliged to conceal the true state of the army from public view, and thereby expose myself to destruction and calumny.

By almost superhuman exertions the army was kept together until spring brought relief in both weather and supplies. The British evacuated Philadelphia early in the morning of June 18, 1778, and commenced their march across Jersey to New York City. The news reached Washington about 10 A.M., and in half an hour three brigades of Continentals were in pursuit; three more brigades followed in the afternoon and the rest of the army early the next morning. The movement was rapid, and six Headquarters were established and broken up in the ten days that ensued before the Continentals overtook and forced the British from the field at Monmouth Court-House. After nightfall the defeated enemy slipped away, and the next day the Continentals turned northward to afford protection to the Hudson Highlands. Moving by easy stages they took three weeks to reach White Plains, New York, the best position from which to block any move by land from New York City. The Headquarters on the way were at Freehold, New Jersey; Englishtown, Spotswood, Brunswick Landing, Paramus, Haverstraw, New York; the Delavan House on the east side of the Hud-

son, and White Plains. Here from the Headquarters at Reuben Wright's Mills, Washington wrote to
Thomas Nelson in Virginia:

It is not a little pleasing, nor less wonderful to contem-
plate, that after two years' maneuvering and undergoing
the strangest vicissitudes, that perhaps ever attended any
one contest since the creation, both armies are brought
back to the very point they set out from, and that which
was the offending party in the beginning is now reduced to
the spade and pickaxe for defense.

Yet, with truth, he could have pushed the parallel
further and likened the retreat of the British across
the Jerseys to the retreat of the Continentals before
them, through that same region in 1776.

A month later, September 23, 1778, Headquarters
were moved to Fredericksburg, where Reed Ferriss's
house first, and later John Kane's, were successively
occupied. Toward the end of November the British
made a display of activity, organized an expedition
and sailed up the Hudson with a show of force. They
proceeded only as far as King's Ferry, however, and,
without attempting anything, returned to New York.
The Headquarters were at Raritan, New Jersey, December 12th, and December 13th at the John Wallace
house at Middlebrook for the winter. Here they remained until June 4th, when the rumored intent of the
British against the Highlands opened the campaign of
1779. June 6th the Headquarters were at Slott's or
Slote's, Orange County, New York; at Smith's Clove
for the next seventeen days, and at New Windsor,

New York, June 23d. Here, at the house of William Ellison, which is no longer standing, they remained until July 20th, when they were established at Moore's house near West Point, there to remain for the next four months, or until November 27th.

Moore's house is another of the Headquarters now no longer in existence. It had been built by John Moore in 1749, and stood about a mile to the north of West Point on ground that is now within the lines of the United States Government reservation. During the time that Washington was at New Windsor the plan against Stony Point was brilliantly executed by Wayne and the Light Infantry, and Headquarters were located at the Point for one day, July 17th. It is from Moore's house also that we have the rare description, from Washington's own pen, of a dinner at Headquarters. August 16, 1779, he wrote to Surgeon-General John Cochran, inviting Mrs. Cochran and Mrs. Livingston to dine with him, describing and apologizing in advance for the meal they would be served.

I have asked Mrs. Cochran & Mrs. Livingston to dine with me tomorrow; but am I not in honor bound to apprize them of their fare? As I hate deception, even where the imagination only is concerned; I will. It is needless to premise that my table is large enough to hold the ladies. Of this they had ocular proof yesterday. To say how it is usually covered, is rather more essential; and this shall be the purport of my letter. Since our arrival at this happy spot, we have had a ham (sometimes a shoulder) of Bacon, to grace the head of the Table; a piece of roast Beef adorns the foot; and a dish of beans, or greens (almost imperceptible) decorates the center. When the cook has a mind to cut a figure (which I presume will be the case tomorrow), we have two Beef-steak pyes, or dishes of crabs, in addition, one on each side the center dish, dividing the space & reducing the distance between dish & dish to about 6 feet, which would without them be near 12 feet apart. Of late he has had the surprising sagacity to discover, that apples will make pyes; and its a question, if, in the violence of his efforts, we do not get one of apples, instead of having both of Beef-steaks. If the ladies can put up with such entertainment, and will submit to partake of it on plates, once Tin but now Iron — (not become so by the labor of scouring), I shall be happy to see them.

On December 3d the Headquarters were moved to Morristown, New Jersey, in the house of Mrs. Theodosia Ford, widow of Jacob Ford, Jr. This house is still standing, and while there the Commander-in-Chief had the house replastered at a cost of £75 and cleaned out and restored the well on the place. Mrs. Ford refused to accept pay for the use of her house. Headquarters remained there until the opening of the campaign of 1780, which started with the British raid on Springfield June 7th. From this date until the army again went into winter quarters little of military value was accomplished, though the troops were almost continuously maneuvering through East Jersey and the Hudson valley in New York. Twenty-two Headquarters were established during this summer and fall during which Washington visited and dis-

cussed plans of coöperation with Comte de Rochambeau, commanding the newly arrived French expeditionary forces, and the despicable treason of Benedict
Arnold failed of its purpose. Of these twenty-two
Headquarters, that in Colonel Theunis Dey's house at
Preakness, New Jersey, from July 1st to July 28th,
was of the longest duration. From Preakness, which
is now the city of Paterson, the Headquarters moved
successively to Paramus; Kakeat, New York, Peekskill, Verplanck's, and Stony Point, where the Hudson
was recrossed at King's Ferry; Clarkstown, Orangetown, or Tappan, where the Headquarters were in the
De Wint house; Teaneck, at the Liberty Pole Tavern,
now Englewood; Kendekamack, September 4th;
Steenrapie, September 5th, where Washington quartered in the Hopper house until the 19th; the next day
again at Orangetown; October 7th again at Paramus,
New Jersey, and at Totawa, in Passaic County, from
October 9th to November 28th, when the Headquarters were moved to New Windsor, New York. Here
they remained until June 24, 1781, in the house of
William Ellison, which is no longer standing. At Ellison's occurred the breach between Washington and
Hamilton, which resulted in the latter's resignation as
aide-de-camp. It was youthful egoism and petulance
smarting under a fancied injustice, and Hamilton's
own description of the occurrence to his father-in-law,
Philip Schuyler, is not entirely to his credit.

In May, 1781, Washington held a second confer-

THE DEY HOUSE
Washington's Headquarters

ence with Rochambeau at Weathersfield, Connecticut, and in June the Continentals moved to effect a junction with the French for an attempt upon New York City. The Headquarters were at Peekskill, Tarrytown, Valentine's Hill, and near Dobb's Ferry. The junction of the two armies was effected July 6th at Phillipsburg, twelve miles from Kingsbridge; the Headquarters remained "near Dobb's Ferry" until the news of De Grasse's fleet settled the plan of the campaign and the march to Virginia was begun August 19th. The allied armies crossed the Hudson at King's Ferry August 20th, and between then and October 1st, when the Commander-in-Chief's quarters were established before Yorktown, but seven Headquarters were created. These were at Haverstraw, New York, August 23d; Ramapo, New Jersey, August 25th; Two Bridges and Chatham, August 26th and 27th; Head of Elk, Maryland; Williamsburg, Virginia; Secretary's Quarter, September 28th, and in the field before Yorktown October 1st. Cornwallis surrendered October 19th, and the next Headquarters from which military orders were issued as such were in Philadelphia, where from December 6, 1781, to March 22, 1782, Washington occupied the house of Benjamin Chew, 110 South Third Street, which is not now standing. On March 31st the Commander-in-Chief arrived at Newburgh, New York, and established Headquarters in the Jonathan Hasbrouck house. This house is still standing and is, perhaps by virtue of its location as well as the length of time it was occupied by the Commander-in-Chief, the best known, next to Valley Forge, of all of Washington's Headquarters.

It was here that Washington so sternly rebuked Colonel Nicola for the suggestion that the army be used to set up a military monarchy, and here that the most dangerous of all insubordinate movements of the Revolution, set on foot by the anonymous Newburgh Addresses, was dissipated and brought to naught by the diplomatic tact of the Commander-in-Chief. On August 31, 1782, the army moved down to Verplanck's Point for the last of the many attempts against the city of New York. In coöperation with the French several parades and reviews of the troops were held, but the situation of affairs and the political aspect of the war did not warrant the losses sure to be incurred in an assault upon the city. October 22d the French allies commenced their march to Boston, there to embark for the West Indies; the Continentals went into winter quarters at New Windsor and Washington returned to the Headquarters at Newburgh. The last orders were issued from here August 17, 1783, and Washington set out for Princeton the next day to appear before Congress in answer to its summons. August 24th he established the last Headquarters of the Revolution at Rocky Hill, New Jersey, four miles north of Princeton, in the house of Mrs. Margaret Berrien, the widow of Judge Berrien. It was at Rocky

Hill that he received the letter from Mrs. Elizabeth Thompson, his old housekeeper during the greater part of the war. It is a letter worthy of a patriotic woman who had struggled to make the Headquarters of the Continental Army as comfortable for the Commander-in-Chief as the meager circumstances of those hard years would admit. On October 10, 1783, she wrote to Washington:

> When I had the honor of seeing your Excellency at Princeton, you desired that I should make out an account for my services in your family to be laid before the Financier. I came into your Excellency's service as housekeeper in the month of June, 1776, with a zealous heart to do the best in my power. Although my abilities had not the strength of my inclinations, your goodness was pleased to approve and bear with me until December, 1781, when age made it necessary for me to retire. Your bounty and goodness at that time bestowed upon me the sum of £179. 6. 8. which makes it impossible for me to render an account; my services were never equal to what your benevolence had thus rated them. . . .

From the Berrien house at Rocky Hill Washington issued his Farewell Orders to the Armies of the United States on Sunday, November 2, 1783, in which house as Commander-in-Chief, he addressed:

> . . . himself once more, and that for the last time, to the armies of the United States (however widely dispersed the individuals who compose them may be), and to bid them an affectionate, a long farewell. But before the Commander-in-Chief takes final leave of those he holds most dear, he wishes to indulge himself a few moments in calling to mind a slight review of the past . . . and he will conclude the ad-

dress by expressing the obligations he feels himself under for the spirited and able assistance he has experienced from them, in the performance of an arduous office ... the unparalleled perseverance of the armies of the United States, through almost every possible suffering and discouragement for the space of eight long years, was little short of a standing miracle. ... Let it be known and remembered that the reputation of the federal armies is established beyond the reach of malevolence; and let a consciousness of their achievements and fame still incite the men, who composed them, to honorable actions ... and, while he congratulates them on the glorious occasion, which renders their services in the field no longer necessary, he wishes to express the strong obligations he feels himself under for the assistance he has received from every class and in every instance. He presents his thanks in the most serious and affectionate manner to the general officers, as well for their counsel on many interesting occasions, as for their ardor in promoting the success of the plans he had adopted; to the commandants of regiments and corps, and to the other officers, for their great zeal and attention in carrying his orders promptly into execution; to the staff, for their alacrity and exactness in performing the duties of their several departments; and to the non-commissioned officers and private soldiers, for their extraordinary patience and suffering, as well as their invincible fortitude in action. To the various branches of the army, the General takes this last and solemn opportunity of professing his inviolable attachment and friendship. ... And being now to conclude these last public orders, to take his ultimate leave in a short time of the military character, and to bid a final adieu to the armies he has so long had the honor to command, he can only again offer in their behalf his recommendations to their grateful country, and his prayers to the God of armies. . . .

No general orders were issued after these of November 2d. A few "garrison" orders at West Point were sent out and the necessary directions given for moving the remnant of the army down to and into New York City as the British withdrew. The last Headquarters of the Revolutionary War, at Rocky Hill, were broken up November 12 or 13, 1783 (the exact date of the event is uncertain), and Washington reached West Point November 14th. Here he remained until, with about a thousand troops, he marched into New York on the 25th of November, 1783.

V

THE AIDES–DE–CAMP OF GENERAL GEORGE WASHINGTON

GEORGE WASHINGTON'S "Family," as he called his aides-de-camp during the Revolutionary War, was the most remarkable group of young men to be found in the history of the United States. Washington's well-nigh unerring judgment in appraising men was never better displayed than in the choice of his confidential military assistants, for, no matter how much of their later success in life is to be attributed to the training they received under the Commander-in-Chief of the Continental Army, there can be no question of the quick recognition, by the First American, of the latent capacity of these men who were so much younger than himself.

This group furnished the Nation with a diplomatic representative to Spain and Portugal, an Associate Justice of the United States Supreme Court, six Cabinet officers (Secretaries of State, of War, of the Treasury, and an Attorney General), three United States Senators, four Governors of States, one Speaker of the House of Representatives, one President of the Continental Congress, and one delegate to the Convention which framed the Constitution of the United States. A goodly list of high and honorable accomplishment! Those who did not attain to distinguished political positions nevertheless became citizens of worth, of local reputation and honor as lawyers, judges, or men of affairs.

Able to judge well and truly the capacities of men, George Washington, in turn, impressed his personality upon all who came in contact with him, and this impress upon the aides reacted unfavorably only upon two out of the entire number. It is interesting to note that the two who later became lukewarm in their personal allegiance were among those who served the shortest time at Headquarters.

There were, in all, thirty-two aides and their periods of service spread over the entire war in such wise that the Headquarters' staff numbered from four to seven aides at all times. From the middle of the year 1776 one aide was always a Military Secretary; there was also an Assistant Secretary, and, from 1780 to the end of the war, there was a Recording Secretary. There were several extra aides; two of these were by special appointment, one was complimentary, with neither rank nor pay, and one, a unique appointment, was by brevet. None of the aides were as old as the Commander-in-Chief and most of them were from ten to fifteen years younger than Washington, who had passed his forty-third birthday when he was unanimously elected, by Congress, to be General and Commander-in-Chief of all the forces raised or to be raised by the United Colonies.

The youngest of the aides, when appointed, was John Trumbull, the artist, who was nineteen years old in 1775; Alexander Hamilton, twenty years old, was the next youngest. Stephen Moylan was the oldest, being but two years younger than the Commander-in-Chief. The length of service, like the ages of the aides, varied considerably. John Trumbull served only twenty days and Tench Tilghman seven years. Robert Hanson Harrison, next to Tilghman, served the longest, with six years of the war to his credit; John Laurens and Richard Kidder Meade both served four years; Hamilton and David Humphreys, three years. The length of service of all the rest averaged from one to two years, excepting the 1775 appointees, Mifflin, Moylan, Randolph, and Reed, whose records stand: Mifflin one month, Moylan four months, Randolph seven, and Reed ten. Two later appointees, Johnston and Walker, also served seven and ten months, respectively.

Seven of the Thirteen States were represented on Washington's staff during the war, but it merely happened thus, for State representation in such connection was unthought of, the main consideration being that of ability. Virginia, as was natural, furnished twelve, the greatest number; there were four each from Massachusetts, New York, and Connecticut; three from Pennsylvania and Maryland, and one each from North and South Carolina. All of the appointments were unsolicited. Some few applications were

made to Washington during the war, but they were disregarded, and, with the exception of Tilghman and John Laurens, son of the President of Congress, both of whom volunteered, the aides were either specifically invited to serve by Washington himself, or were sent to the Commander-in-Chief by his close friends with what he considered proper recommendation and under proper auspices.

Washington was elected to command the army June 15, 1775; he accepted the appointment the next day and his commission, a beautifully proportioned and designed parchment, engrossed by Timothy Matlack, was signed by President John Hancock, June 19th. On June 16th Congress authorized the appointment of a Secretary to the Commander-in-Chief at a salary of sixty-six dollars a month. June 21st it was resolved to allow all generals of the army three aides-de-camp, for whom the pay had been fixed previously at thirty-three dollars per month. On June 23d Washington set out for the army at Cambridge accompanied, among others, by the two Pennsylvanians, Thomas Mifflin and Joseph Reed. July 3d he assumed command of the troops, and the next day the military "Family" of the Commander-in-Chief came into existence for the period of the war by the announcement, in general orders, of the appointment of Joseph Reed, Military Secretary, and Thomas Mifflin, Aide-de-camp. A glimpse of the real George Washington is furnished us in the appointment of the next aide.

Young John Trumbull, the artist, furnished valuable assistance to Washington by means of his clever sketch maps of the British lines and defenses around Boston, and no man could better appreciate such work than the Commander-in-Chief, whose own survey drawing was of fine quality. Trumbull was appointed an aide July 27th. He served at Headquarters until the middle of August, and was then transferred to the staff of General Gates. He resigned from the army in 1777, but volunteered and served as an aide to Major-General John Sullivan in the disastrous Rhode Island expedition of 1778. He managed to get to France in 1780, and, in furtherance of his art studies, determined to go to London for instruction under Benjamin West. His artistic naïveté was rudely jarred when the British put him in jail. There he stayed for eight months, and was released only on condition that he leave the kingdom. The calmness with which this ex-aide of the rebel Commander-in-Chief walked into the lion's mouth merely because he wished to study art was regarded, probably, by the British as the act of a lunatic. It was, in truth, only a bit of evidence of the quality of the manhood opposed to them, and it should have shown Great Britain her utter misunderstanding of the character of the American colonists and her gross misconception of the American spirit.

Thomas Mifflin resigned to become Quartermaster General of the army the day before Trumbull left

Headquarters, and these two vacancies were filled by Edmund Randolph and George Baylor, both from Virginia and young men of twenty-two and twenty-three years of age, respectively. Randolph was the nephew of Peyton Randolph, a former President of the Continental Congress, and, on the death of his uncle in March, 1776, he was forced to leave the army and return to Virginia. Baylor left Headquarters in January, 1777, to become colonel of the Third Continental Dragoons. He was bayoneted through the lungs when his command was surprised by the British at Tappan. He lived throughout the war and saw further service, but this bayonet wound was the cause of his untimely death.

During the siege of Boston the larger part of the work of the aides was secretarial, drafting and recording letters and orders and keeping track of affairs. It was not a new thing with Washington, for his experience as Commander-in-Chief on the Virginia frontier during the French and Indian War had accustomed him to managing bodies of troops scattered over a considerable area; but his aides had had no such experience to steady them. In addition to the usual army Headquarters work, matters were complicated by the management of a fleet of privateering vessels which Washington arranged for before the establishment of a regular naval force. Some of the aides were obliged to travel to the seacoast on this business, and it fell to the lot of Stephen Moylan to keep track of most of this naval activity.

The record of the correspondence at Headquarters at the beginning of the war was entered up in cheap blank books, with covers of unsized, blue paper, just as the letters happened to be written, minus all indexing, devoid of line spacing, and classified only into two rather vague groups of official and private letters. This was a clumsy and unsatisfactory method, and, though the books start off neatly and fairly enough, hurry and carelessness soon jumbled them into a much confused record. The handwriting of all the aides of the period appear in these letter book records, and it seems plain that certain lines of correspondence were in charge of certain aides. The Commander-in-Chief, of course, signed most of the letters, and, when he did not, it was carefully stated that they were written by his order. As the war continued the volume of Headquarters' correspondence increased to enormous proportions, and this letter book method, with which the start was made, proved hopelessly inadequate by the middle of the year 1776. It was entirely discarded after October of that year, and the record of the letters written thereafter was preserved in the form of tentative and corrected drafts, or copies, on separate sheets of paper, that were afterwards folded and docketed for filing.

These drafts and copies were stored in special chests that formed a part of the valuable baggage of Headquarters, and their guardianship was entrusted to the Commander-in-Chief's Guard. Washington's solicitude for their safety is of record in more than one instance, for no one realized better than he the tremendous value of those papers to the conduct of the war and how necessary it was to prevent any of them from falling into the hands of the enemy.

The secretarial method at Headquarters varied. The Commander-in-Chief wrote a large number of the letters himself, and these, if not corrected or changed by him in the course of the composition, were copied off for the record by an aide. If changes were made, a clean copy was prepared for his signature and the corrected draft filed for record; for the rest Washington either gave verbal instructions to the aide or made a few rough notes from which a letter was composed for his signature. One or two of these rough memoranda still survive.

The statement, for which Timothy Pickering seems largely responsible, that Washington was not a good letter-writer, and that most of his communications were the work of his aides, is not borne out by a study of the drafts. It is true that the greater number of these drafts are in the handwritings of the various aides, but the alterations, suppressions, and additions in Washington's handwriting are numerous, and in every such instance the change strengthens and improves the aide's composition.

A fair example of the control and dominance of the Commander-in-Chief over his correspondence is found in the draft of the letter to Major-General Horatio

Gates of May 26, 1778. Gates, in command in the north, had summarily countermanded Washington's orders for shipment of arms to the main army, then at Valley Forge. There were fully two thousand troops there in want of muskets, and the British, only a few miles away in Philadelphia, might move at any moment. Tench Tilghman, burning with rage at Gates's impertinence and dangerous action, drafted, for Washington's signature, a stinging rebuke and peremptory order to the hero of Saratoga. But the Commander-in-Chief, keenly alive to Gates's frame of mind as a result of the then recent fiasco of the Conway Cabal, struck out all of the peremptory part of the letter and shifted the rebuke from the personal plane, upon which it had been placed by Tilghman, to the higher line of official duty. Tilghman had written, for Washington: "This countermand has greatly disappointed and exceedingly distressed me." Washington struck out the personal pronoun and changed the sentence to read: "This countermand has greatly disappointed and exceedingly distressed and injured the service." Pickering is not an entirely unbiased judge regarding Washington.

One cannot read any considerable number of Washington's letters without catching the undeviating and uniform swing and spirit of them, and this uniformity could not be so apparent if thirty-one different personalities, as strongly positive as were the aides, had controlled the correspondence over a period of eight years.

That Washington did not disdain to avail himself of the ability of his aides is unquestioned. It was beyond the power of any single individual to have carried, unaided, the burden that rested on his shoulders while Commander-in-Chief of the Continental Army; but if his aides gave him valuable assistance and support, the more honor to them for their co-operation, rather than the less credit to Washington for his achievements. Certainly the personal devotion and enthusiasm of the men who lived on daily intimate terms with George Washington was not cooled by carping criticism or grudging service.

The first year of the war saw Washington's staff increased from one Military Secretary and one aide to five aides, and, by the end of the year, the multiplicity of duties and the heavy correspondence had become so great that Washington asked Congress for authority to appoint more aides, assuring that body that he did not mean to run the public into unnecessary expense and that he would be as sparing as possible in his appointments. Congress took no steps in the matter and, what with resignations and replacements, the year 1776 started with four aides and one Military Secretary; nine aides were added during the year and six dropped out. In January, Congress, blandly ignoring Washington's request for more aides, asked his opinion as to the rank his aides should have, and, in response to his recommendation, conferred upon them that of major. In June this rank was raised to that of lieutenant-colonel, and it so remained throughout the war.

In May, 1776, Washington was empowered to appoint an assistant clerk to his Military Secretary (who was then Robert Hanson Harrison, of Virginia, successor to Joseph Reed), at a salary of forty-four dollars a month; in July authority was granted to appoint another aide. But the pressure of work had become too great to wait upon the tortoise-like action of Congress, and the Commander-in-Chief found a makeshift way out of the difficulty by appointing two of the officers of his Guard as Special Aides; one was his young relative, George Lewis, a lieutenant of the Guard, and the other was Major Caleb Gibbs, its Commandant. Both of these were continually at Headquarters in the performance of their Guard duties, so it was a practical solution. It increased the burdens of these two officers, but there were no slackers around General George Washington, who spared himself as little as he spared men, horses, and material, when necessity demanded that a thing be done.

Congress slept on the matter of increasing the number of the aides until January, 1778, when it finally did what it should have done in the beginning and what it always did do at the end of every vexatious military question, that is, threw the entire responsibility on the shoulders of the Commander-in-Chief, by granting him authority to appoint such a number of aides as he might, from time to time, judge necessary.

Regimental officers could be so appointed, any resolve of Congress to the contrary notwithstanding. The Commander-in-Chief was furnished with blank commissions, signed and sealed by the President and Secretary of Congress with authority to fill them out as he saw fit, and his succeeding appointments were never called into question.

Robert Hanson Harrison had been appointed Military Secretary in November, 1775; Alexander Contee Hanson, of Maryland, and William Grayson, of Virginia, were appointed Assistant Secretaries on the same day in June, 1776. Harrison, as has been stated, succeeded Reed, the first Secretary, and was one of the quartet of best known and longest service aides; Moylan, Palfrey, Cary, and Webb were added to the staff, and a French merchant, Pierre Penet, was given the rank of aide by brevet. Congress confirmed this brevet appointment by Washington and a commission was forwarded to France, from whence Penet had applied by letter to the Commander-in-Chief, for the honor. This was the unique staff appointment of the war. Penet and his business partner, Emanuel de Pliarne, came to America in 1775 and conferred with Washington at Cambridge; from thence they went to Philadelphia, where they conferred with a committee of Congress. On their return to France, Penet made the request for a commission so as to have the privilege of wearing the Continental uniform and ribbon of rank in France. His letter to Washington is guarded in language, but explicit in stating that he had succeeded in making arrangements for furnishing ample supplies of ammunition for Washington's armies and garrisons. Unfortunately there seems to be no documentary evidence available, as yet, that enables us to fix the value of the services rendered by Penet & Pliarne, or Penet & Company; but it must have been actual and substantial or Washington would hardly have granted so unusual an honor. The idea was that Penet, in France, could the more readily arrange for supplies for the army in America when clad in the Continental uniform, and Washington certainly thought the scheme worthy of trial. Whether this ardent Frenchman was the advance agent of Caron de Beaumarchais or was connected in any way with the latter's enterprise remains to be established.

The same year that this unusual appointment was made a young Marylander, by the name of Tench Tilghman, appeared at Headquarters. He was not unknown to Congress, as he had been secretary to the commissioners who had negotiated the treaty of 1775 with the Six Nations of Indians. He had been a lieutenant in a Philadelphia militia company and, after the Indian treaty work, had joined the fighting forces of his country. In August, 1776, he volunteered to serve at Headquarters without rank or pay. There were many volunteers in the different branches of both the civil and military service during the Revolutionary War, but few can show a more honorable and highly patriotic record than that of Tench Tilghman. When he joined Headquarters, shortly before the battle of Long Island, he was thirty-two years old, and for the next seven years he gave the best of his strength and abilities to his country with a prodigality that ended his life ten years from the time he appeared at Headquarters.

Alexander Hamilton, ot New York, and Richard Kidder Meade, of Virginia, became aides in 1777 and, with Harrison and Tilghman, bore the heaviest of the Headquarters' burdens for the longest period of the war. The aides were by natural characteristics and by a kind of understanding among themselves, divided into two groups, or classes: the "writing" and the "riding" aides. The distinction was not always clean-cut as there never was a group of men so willing to spend themselves without stint as these confidential assistants of General George Washington.

Robert Hanson Harrison, for all that he was a secretary, was the best-known of the "riding" aides, and his powerful black mare was almost as well known to the army as were the splendid mounts of the Commander-in-Chief. Hamilton was both a "riding" and a "writing" aide, but Tilghman was primarily the "writing" man. Nearly all of the aides were good penmen, but Hamilton and Tilghman may be considered the best. Hamilton undoubtedly was the finest penman of them all, and when he took pains his script is a perfect Spencerian. The commission of

March 4, 1777, appointing his fellow aide, Harrison, a commissioner to negotiate an exchange of prisoners with the British, has the beauty and accuracy of a copper-plate engraving. The reason for the pains taken with this paper is clear; Harrison had to present this document to the British commissioners, as his credentials, and Hamilton's pride in the Continental Army was such that he took great pains to show the enemy that there was as much skill and art among the Continentals as among the king's troops.

It was to Hamilton also that the drafting of the more important letters was entrusted, and Washington's changes and improvements of Hamilton's compositions are, comparatively, few; still there are a sufficient number of them to show the Commander-in-Chief's letter-writing ability, for, in Hamilton's case, as in that of every other aide, Washington never changed their sentences but that he did not strengthen and better them. Major Caleb Gibbs who, in addition to his duties as commandant of the Commander-in-Chief's Guard, acted as superintendent of household affairs at Headquarters, drafted or copied many letters when the need was great. Any one who happened to be present was pressed into service as an amanuensis, and no less a personage than Major-General Greene helped out at times in copying needed enclosures for letters, while some few of the record copies were made by Mrs. Washington when she was at Headquarters. The haste and pressure of work at times is clearly shown by the drafts of some of the longer letters being in the handwriting of two or three aides as one after another of them were called away for more imperative work.

There have been many unauthentic and inaccurate lists of Washington's aides published, and so many unsubstantiated claims of service are continually being made that the accurate and complete list may have both interest and value. For the names that follow, a general order, a resolve of Congress, or a definite documentary statement by the Commander-in-Chief is the only recognized authority:

Thomas Mifflin, of Pennsylvania, July 4, 1775; Joseph Reed, of Pennsylvania, Secretary, July 4, 1775; John Trumbull, Connecticut, July 27, 1775; George Baylor, Virginia, August 15, 1775; Edmund Randolph, Virginia, August 15, 1775; Robert Hanson Harrison, Virginia, November 5, 1775, Secretary, May 16, 1776; Stephen Moylan, Pennsylvania, March 5, 1776; William Palfrey, Massachusetts, March 6, 1776; Caleb Gibbs, Massachusetts, special appointment, May 16, 1776; George Lewis, Virginia, special appointment, May 16, 1776; Richard Cary, Virginia, June 21, 1776; Samuel Blatchley Webb, Connecticut, June 21, 1776; Alexander Contee Hanson, Maryland, Assistant Secretary, June 21, 1776; William Grayson, Virginia, Assistant Secretary, June 21, 1776; Pierre Penet, France, by brevet, confirmed by Congress, October 14, 1776; John Fitzgerald, Virginia, November, 1776; George Johnston, Virginia, January 20, 1777; John Walker, North Carolina, extra aide, February 19, 1777; Alexander Hamilton, New York, March 1, 1777; Richard Kidder Meade, Virginia, March 12, 1777; Presley Peter Thornton, Virginia, extra aide, September 6, 1777; John Laurens, South Carolina, volunteer extra aide, September 6, 1777, given rank March 29, 1779; James McHenry, Maryland, Assistant Secretary, May 15, 1778; Tench Tilghman, Maryland, June 21, 1780.(Tilghman had, however, been serving as volunteer aide without rank or pay since August, 1776); David Humphreys, Connecticut, June 23, 1780; Richard Varick, New York, Recording Secretary, May 25, 1781; Jonathan Trumbull, Jr., Connecticut, Secretary, June 8, 1781; David Cobb, Massachusetts, June 15, 1781; Peregrine Fitzhugh, Virginia, extra aide, July 2, 1781; William Stephens Smith, New York, July 6, 1781; Benjamin Walker, New York, January 25, 1782; Hodijah Baylies, Massachusetts, extra aide, May 14, 1782.

During the Yorktown campaign John Parke Custis served as a volunteer aide, but without rank, pay, or appointment, so that he cannot properly be included in the above list.

Life at Headquarters was an exciting one; the aides were a hard-riding, hard-working little group, and it was oftentimes due to the driving energy with which they delivered the Commander-in-Chief's orders that Washington's plans were successfully carried through.

But, hard-working as they were, it is questionable if any of them were as unsparing of themselves as was their General. The amount of work accomplished at Headquarters was enormous; often in the height of a campaign a dozen or more letters a day were written at Headquarters. Let any one try to write from eight to twelve letters in long hand, on vitally important matters, of from one to four folio pages in length, to Congress, to Governors of States or State Legislatures, to commanding and subordinate officers of an army, issue general orders for managing a force of from ten to fifteen thousand men, keep in the saddle for hours, enter up a daily expense account, sign warrants for the disbursement of hundreds of dollars of public funds, plan and continually revise plans for a military campaign, while striving always to keep an army supplied with food, clothing, and arms, and on top of all this, make perhaps a forced march and fight a battle, and it easily can be seen that George Washington could have obtained hardly more than three consecutive hours of sleep in any twenty-four, during the eight years of the Revolutionary War. Had he not been a physical giant (he was about six feet two inches tall and weighed two hundred and ten pounds), he could never have stood such a strain.

The demands upon the aides at all times were varied. Almost at the beginning of the war came a peculiarly petty attempt by the British to ignore official recognition of the Continental Army by obtaining the acceptance of a letter from the British Commander-in-Chief, addressed to "George Washington, Esquire." This was checkmated by Joseph Reed, who flatly refused to receive the letter from the flag of truce bearer. Feigning ignorance, the British flag officer asked how such communications should be addressed, but Reed cleverly avoided a possible pitfall and replied that his general's name and rank were well known, and that the proper form of address could easily be imagined. The effect of the little encounter was sufficient; all further letters to Washington from the British authorities bore a proper address. A more important diplomatic accomplishment was the mission of Hamilton, who with Caleb Gibbs traveled through the biting, winter weather of upper New York State to obtain needed reinforcements for Washington from Gates, after the Saratoga victory, when the latter no longer needed a large force. Gates, puffed up with vainglorious pride, talked largely of a winter campaign against Ticonderoga and delayed obeying Washington's orders. Hamilton by sheer mental dominance succeeded in dragging Morgan's splendid rifle regiment from Gates's reluctant grasp, and by pressure in other directions, combined with a bit of luck, succeeded in forwarding State troops and militia enough to Washington, without displaying the plenary power with which he had been invested. To have overridden Gates at that particular time and by such means might have split the army into factions and caused great mischief to the colonial cause. Of all of Hamilton's triumphs of management, it is doubtful if any of those in his after life exceeded the careful genius and self-repression of this youthful diplomacy.

Some of the more pleasant features of life at Headquarters were the times when the army was in winter quarters and Mrs. Washington visited the General. It was the duty of one of the aides to meet her, usually a hundred miles or so away, and escort her to camp. When spring approached and the army took the field again, Mrs. Washington returned to Mount Vernon, and an aide accompanied her on the way until all the country, in which there was danger from the enemy, had been passed. It may easily be assumed that the honor and pleasure of this escort duty was a coveted one with the aides.

But there were many distasteful as well as pleasant experiences in the busy days at Headquarters, and one of these is pictured for us in a succinct and grimly vivid way by Major Caleb Gibbs. In his diary, which he kept in an exasperatingly haphazard way, is this account of the execution of Major John André, the Adjutant General of the British Army. Under date of October 2, 1780, Gibbs wrote:

At 12 o'clock P.M. Major Andrie, Adjt.Genl. to the B.Army was executed persuant to his sentence determined by a board of Genl. Officers. As soon as he got into the cart he said with a firm composure of mind "that he was perfectly reconciled to his Death, but not quite to the mode" — he look around & adres'd himself to the officer of the

Guard & said with a smile "It is but for a moment, Sir" he
seem not in the least agitated in his last moments, not one
moment before he was turn off he was asked if he had any
[thing] to say as time would be allowed him for that purpose he said nothing more than he call on all the gentlemen
present to bear witness that he died like a brave man — &
did.

There are many curious and interesting sidelights
to be found in an examination of the Revolutionary
War from the standpoint of the work of the aides-de-
camp to the Commander-in-Chief. In winter quarters, or in the field, under fire, they were the men upon
whom Washington first placed dependence, and there
is no record of a failure of that dependence. The aides,
apparently, were allowed considerable latitude in
management, and the working arrangements at
Headquarters seem to have been left entirely to
them. With the advent of each new aide into the
"Family" all the drudgery of writing seems to have
been bequeathed him at once by the older aides, and
the new man's gradual emancipation from the more
confining tasks, as he became accustomed to the situation, can be followed easily in the record drafts of the
Headquarters' papers. The aides examined deserters and prisoners, checked accounts, kept record of
the warrants drawn and sums received from the
Paymaster-General, carried and delivered orders,
translated the French and Spanish letters, arranged
for the location of Headquarters, were the *liaison* officers between the Continental Army and the French

1780 2. At 12 o'Clock P.M. Major André
Adj't Gen'l to the B. Army was executed
pursuant to his sentence determined
by a board of Gen'l Officers." as soon
as he got into the cart" he said
with a firm composure of mind
"that he was perfectly reconciled to
his death but not quite to the
mode. he look round & addressed
himself to the officer of the guard
& said with a smile, "It is but for
a moment Sir, he seem not in the
least to agitated in his last moments
yet one moment before he was turn off
he was asked if he had any to say as
time would be allowed him for that
purpose he said nothing more than he
"call on all the gentlemen present
"to bear witness that he died like a brave
man — & did

PAGE OF THE DIARY OF CALEB GIBBS DESCRIBING THE
EXECUTION OF MAJOR ANDRÉ

auxiliary troops, and managed the Headquarters correspondence, this last in itself a colossal task.

There was but one aide who parted from Washington in anger, and that one was Hamilton. Imperious by nature and quick-tempered in the extreme, without the control that later years brought to him, Hamilton resigned in a huff in 1780. Both men were somewhat to blame; Washington seems to have displayed some of the petulance so usual with advancing years and Hamilton the quick resentment of hot youth; but that Washington bore no grudge and that Hamilton was ashamed of his hastiness is quite evident from the lifelong friendship that afterwards existed between the two men. The Marquis de Lafayette was the unconscious cause of the rupture, and this, undoubtedly, had much to do with Washington's willingness to forget the incident. He unbent almost immediately and did all that could reasonably be expected toward adjusting matters; it was Hamilton's obstinacy and youthful pride that forced the separation, and this places the greater share of the blame upon his shoulders. The correspondence between the two men, a short while thereafter, when Hamilton wished to return to the army, is well worth reading. There was the unsurmountable difficulty of seniority of rank, so Hamilton promptly volunteered and had the supreme satisfaction of commanding one of the storming parties against the British redoubts at Yorktown.

Another incident of great interest in the story of the

"Family" is an example of Washington's high sense of justice and sensitiveness to the honor of a fellow soldier. Richard Varick, aide-de-camp to Benedict Arnold at the time of Arnold's treason, though cleared by court-martial of all complicity in the matter, found himself still an object of suspicion to his fellow countrymen. He asked Washington to publish the findings of his trial and to add a certificate as to Varick's character, to stop the mouth of slander. Washington had neither the money nor the authority to do such a thing, but he had been considering, for some time, the need and advantage of having the huge mass of his papers at Headquarters properly classified and arranged. The bulk of them was great and there had been no time in which to file them with system. He could not comply with Varick's request, but he did infinitely better, he obtained the sanction of Congress to employ a Recording Secretary, and he appointed Richard Varick to the position.

As Recording Secretary, Varick had complete charge and control of all the confidential records of the army. Against such proof of Washington's confidence no slanderous whisper could live. The magnificent piece of work performed by Varick and the clerks employed by him still exists in the form of forty-four folio volumes of beautiful penmanship, of three hundred or more pages each, that are known to historians as the "Varick Transcript" and are of lasting value to American history.

There is not a name in the entire list of aides that does not bear with it an honorable record of patriotic service, and every one of those young men is deserving of having his name forever linked with that of the Commander-in-Chief of the Continental Army. Every one of them was appreciated and well liked by his General, and every one of them received, at one time or another during his service, some mark of commendation from Washington. The highest honor granted to any aide during the war was conferred upon Tench Tilghman. The day Cornwallis surrendered, Tilghman vaulted into the saddle and galloped north for Philadelphia, bearing Washington's official despatches announcing to Congress the victory that ended the war. Shortly after midnight of the fourth day, Tilghman rode into the city. It was rapid traveling from the Virginia peninsula, and, in the early morning hours, Congress, the city, and later the Nation awoke to the realization that the war was over and independence won.

Congress voted Tilghman a horse, properly caparisoned, and an elegant sword, in testimony of its opinion of his merit and ability; but the greatest honor had already been conferred upon him when Washington selected him to carry the news of such a victory to the Government. David Humphreys was later sent to deliver to Congress the British flags captured at Yorktown, and Congress rewarded him with a sword. George Baylor and John Laurens had formerly been honored by Congress. Baylor was voted a horse, properly caparisoned, when he brought the news of the Trenton victory, and Laurens was voted a commission as lieutenant-colonel, and Washington was instructed to give him a command as soon as a proper one was available. This honor Laurens declined. He was then serving as a volunteer on the staff at Headquarters, and in due course he was regularly commissioned a lieutenant-colonel and aide-de-camp. These four were the only aides granted honors by Congress.

Three of the aides were wounded while serving at Headquarters. Samuel Blatchley Webb was shot twice: once at White Plains and once at Trenton; John Fitzgerald was wounded at Monmouth, and Laurens was wounded both at Germantown and Monmouth. Webb may be considered the unlucky aide. He had been wounded at Bunker Hill, later at White Plains, and next at Trenton; he became colonel of one of the Sixteen Additional Continental Regiments after leaving Headquarters and was captured by the British and remained a prisoner of war for three years before he could obtain an exchange.

After Yorktown little of a military nature remained to be done, and, though the war dragged on for two years more, the inevitable end was plain, even to Great Britain. Washington purposely avoided bringing on another capital engagement in the field with its consequent loss of life to no better end than that which was already assured, and even the French army left America a year before peace was finally declared.

Washington's military "Family" disbanded at Annapolis, Maryland, December 23, 1783, when the Commander-in-Chief resigned his commission in an address, the formality of which gives little indication of the feeling beneath the measured words. In that address Washington pays the tribute of public acknowledgment to his aides in these words:

> While I repeat my obligations to the army in general, I should do injustice to my own feelings not to acknowledge in this place the peculiar services and distinguished merits of the gentlemen who have been attached to my person during the war. It was impossible the choice of confidential officers to compose my family should have been more fortunate. Permit me, Sir, to recommend in particular those who have continued in the service to the present moment, as worthy of the favorable patronage of Congress.

Humphreys, Cobb, and Walker were with the General on the day of his resignation; rode with him from Annapolis to Mount Vernon and were guests at Washington's first Christmas at home for eight years. Unexpectedly to them the General advanced one hundred dollars to each to help defray the traveling expenses to their homes. They set out December 28th. Trotting down the private road to the Alexandria turnpike, they checked their horses at the gate, to look back across the snow-covered lawn, and it seems most fitting that the final picture of the Revolutionary War should be that of three aides-de-camp, clad in their faded Continental uniforms, waving farewell to the tall figure of the Commander-in-Chief, framed in the doorway of historic Mount Vernon.

VI

GENERAL WASHINGTON'S VALLEY FORGE
EXPENSES

THIS is the story of Washington's Headquarters at
Valley Forge, a story, heretofore untold, of the most
famous of all headquarters of the United States Army,
as told by the expense account, a homely, day-by-day
record, kept in a hand-ruled folio volume by Captain
Caleb Gibbs, Commandant of the Commander-in-
Chief's Guard.

The Continental Army reached the camp site
known as Valley Forge, December 19, 1777. The
troops marched up the old Gulph Road and filed off to
the right and left on the slopes of the rising ground
that forms the true valley by pitching sharply down
to Valley Creek from an undulating crest of two hundred to three hundred and fifty feet in height. Strictly
speaking, the army was not at Valley Forge, but encamped on the slopes in front of the crested heights
forming the valley. The lines formed the arc of a
great circle, swung from the west bank of the Schuylkill to the southern face of Mount Joy, its flanks protected by the river and the mountain. Only Washington's Headquarters and the Commander-in-Chief's
Guard, which was composed entirely of Virginians,
were located in the valley proper. The outer line of
entrenchments was along the crest of a two-hundred-

foot rise. They would have been difficult to carry by
assault; but, whatever the issue here, the inner line, a
mile beyond, flanked by the Washington and Huntington redoubts and just below the crest and eastern
shoulder of Mount Joy, was practically impregnable.
To-day the most impressive feature of Valley Forge is
this line of sunken earthworks that speaks in unmistakable terms of the grim and desperate determination of the Army of the Revolution to stick to the
bitter end.

On Christmas Day the Commander-in-Chief moved
from his tent near the Artillery Park, over the crest of
the rise and down into the real valley to the house
of Deborah Hewes, near the mouth of Valley Creek.
Up to now the Valley Forge Headquarters has been
known as the Isaac Potts House, but this is an undeserved honor. Despite the cheap sentimentality of
the prayer story, proof is lacking that Isaac Potts was
at Valley Forge that winter, and proof is lacking that
he owned, in 1777–78, the house now pointed out as
Headquarters. The accounts show that Deborah
Hewes was paid by Washington for the use of her
house and furniture at Valley Forge, and it is an injustice to Mistress Hewes that she, up to now, has
been ignored. Isaac Potts only came into possession
of the house near the end of the war, and not until
forty years afterwards was the place pointed out as
Washington's Headquarters. By then Potts's long
residence had fixed it in the minds of the country folk

WASHINGTON'S HEADQUARTERS AT VALLEY FORGE

as the Potts House. Rightfully it should be known as the Hewes House, and Mistress Deborah's name should be recalled instead of the Quaker Isaac's.

The first matters of interest encountered in the expense book are the purchases immediately preceding December 25th, from which it is possible to construct Washington's Christmas dinner. There are no entries of expenditures from December 9th to December 22d, while the army was on the march, and, as the settled accounts on December 24th for the period from December 8th show an expenditure of only £9 18*s.* (about $25), there could have been no great surplus of provision in the hands of Steward Patrick McGuire on December 22d. Here is the pitiful account from December 22d to December 24th:

		£	s.	d.
22d	To 4 lb butter, @ 7/6.30/ — To Cabbage 3/9........	1	13	9
	To potatoes 2/6 — To Turnips 2/.................		4	6
	To 2 turkeys @ 12/6. 25/ — To 2 geese @ 10/.20/....	2	5	0
	To 4 fouls @ 4/ .16/ — To 24 lb mutton @ 1/2 .28/..	2	4	0
24th	To turnips 3/9 — To potatoes 2/6.................		6	3
	To 3 lb butter @ 7/6. 22/6 — To 4 fouls @ 3/9.15/...	1	17	6
	To 48 lb veal @ 1/1. 52/.........................	2	12	0

It is from these supplies that the Christmas dinner was provided. First, as to the number of persons to be fed and the quantities available. Each day the general and field officers of the day dined with the Commander-in-Chief at Headquarters by the standing invitation in general orders of November 7, 1777. These officers were five in number — the major-general of the day, the brigadier-general, two lieutenant-colonels, and a brigade major. At Valley Forge Washington's staff, or "military family" as he called it, consisted of nine aides-de-camp; so, counting the Commander-in-Chief, his aides and the officers of the day, there were fifteen men at the table. Besides this number there were eight or ten servants — the steward, housekeeper, cook, washerwoman, hostlers, helpers, and others, so that in the calculation of food consumption an allowance should be made for from twenty to twenty-five persons per day. Of course all of these, including the officers, were entitled to the ration, which, as then established, was one and one quarter pounds of beef, one and one quarter pounds of flour, one half gill of rum, and one half pint of rice per day with certain substitutes; but being entitled to rations and being able to draw them at Valley Forge were two very different things. A report of December 23d showed that there were only twenty-five barrels of flour in camp and no beef, so there could have been little or no help from the commissary for the table at Headquarters even if the Commander-in-Chief would have availed himself of it at such a period of scarcity. From the items noted in the accounts, therefore, must be subtracted the quantities eaten by fifteen to twenty-five healthy, hungry adults in the nine meals before three o'clock in the afternoon of Christmas Day — the dinners and suppers of December 22d, 23d, and 24th, and the breakfasts of December 23d, 24th, and 25th. Can what was left be imagined?

These were the men who sat at table the afternoon
of Christmas Day while the heavy snow drifted down
the gloomy little valley and banked in wet, clinging
masses against frame and sill: George Washington,
grave of mien and towering in physique even among
the stalwarts of the Revolution; on his right the guest
of honor, the Marquis de Lafayette; the Baron de
Kalb, Major-General of the day; Brigadier-General
John Paterson, of New Jersey; Lieutenant-Colonels
Thomas Paxton, of the Pennsylvania militia, and
Robert Ballard, of the Virginia line; and Brigade-
Major Simon Learned, of Massachusetts. The aides-
de-camp were Robert Hanson Harrison, John Fitzgerald, Alexander Hamilton, Richard Kidder Meade,
Presley Peter Thornton, John Laurens, and Tench
Tilghman; all lieutenant-colonels except Tilghman,
the volunteer, who was giving his talents and health
to the cause of liberty without thought or care for
rank or pay. There were two others, acting aides
by special appointments, Captain Caleb Gibbs and
George Lewis, a lieutenant in the Guard and a well-
liked nephew of the Commander-in-Chief. A goodly
company! The young courtier from the most brilliant
court in Europe, the seasoned and critically sardonic
French veteran, an embryo judge of a supreme court,
a future Secretary of the Treasury, and a special am-
bassador to Europe among the young aides who were
learning, as were the others, the greatest lessons of
life from the quiet, dominant figure at the head of

the table. A hundred Valley Forges could not have broken the spirit of American manhood within the candlelight of that board.

And the dinner was this: A little veal, a little mutton; not much, for it is probable that the turkeys, geese, and "fouls" were husbanded for the occasion; a small quantity of potatoes and cabbage and less of turnips. That was all! No tea, no coffee, no milk; a small amount of butter, perhaps, but no bread, no eggs, no flour, so there were no pies, puddings, or dessert. If there was either whiskey or rum, which is doubtful, as none was issued to the troops that day, there was no punch, for sugar was lacking. A minor, though irritating, difficulty was the probable lack of sufficient knives, forks, and spoons, for Washington had been separated from his baggage during the Brandywine and Germantown maneuvers and did not obtain it again until the middle of January.

The prices paid for the food of this Christmas dinner did not vary greatly from present-day values. Reckoning the Pennsylvania shilling at about thirteen and one third cents of the present day, which was, probably, well above its purchasing value, mutton and veal cost about fifteen cents a pound; potatoes a little over a dollar a bushel; turnips about a dollar and a half a bushel, and cabbages thirteen and one third cents apiece. Butter was a dollar a pound, when obtainable, and the chickens, which Gibbs always wrote as "fouls," were fifty cents each, with the turkeys a dollar and a half and the geese a dollar and a quarter each. Two days after Christmas the scant supply of potatoes, turnips, and cabbage was brightened by the advent of a few timid carrots, about thirty cents' worth, to be exact, and it requires dexterous mental arithmetic to figure how these could be fairly apportioned among fifteen hungry men. How the servants existed is an unsolved mystery. The last day in the year one pitiful rabbit was secured, and the day after New Year's the Commander-in-Chief received a present of rock-fish. From whom it came is unknown, but as the man who brought it was given a gratuity of fifteen shillings, the amount of enthusiasm the fish aroused at Headquarters may be imagined. The second week in January something like a real supply of vegetables arrived, as the entry is broadly general:

To cabbage — fouls and onions.............72s. 6

These were the first onions seen at Valley Forge. More arrived the last of the month, and from then on the supply, if not great, was fairly continuous. Meat at Headquarters, when obtainable, was veal and mutton, with such changes as chickens, geese, turkeys, and ducks as could be found. A dozen partridges once graced the table, a pair of pigeons and a wild goose at another time; a piece of smoked venison is recorded in March, by the middle of which month hams, fresh pork, and some smoked beef were obtained. Eggs did not figure in the daily supplies until after Mrs. Washington's arrival in camp, and whether the regularity of the egg purchases after that time was due to her or to the fact that they were then more easily obtained, cannot be determined. Butter came in with greater regularity and in increasing quantity after her arrival, though the lack of salt in the country is evident from the numerous entries for "fresh" butter that appear in the accounts. Mrs. Washington's influence is plainly seen in the record. Even before her arrival, a general sprucing-up of Headquarters is noticeable in the account book. The purchase of five brooms is not only a candid confession of the condition of Headquarters, but an eloquent tribute to Washington's knowledge of his wife's housekeeping standards. A broom for the stable was also bought, and a touch of the cavalier courtier is seen in the purchase of a brush for the General's horses. Washington was rated among the best horsemen of his day, but care of his animals with him was secondary to utility. He seems always to have considered them a means to the end, and seldom spared speed or endurance when necessity arose. Evidence of this is seen in the purchase, in February, of "antimony for the genl's horses" — a stock remedy of olden times for hard-driven, nerve-strained animals.

After Christmas the next entries in the accounts of more than usual interest are those around February 22d, Washington's birthday. On this day the dinner was graced by the first parsnips of the season. Mr. Jameson, probably Colonel John Jameson, at White-marsh, sent a present of "fouls," and Colonel Clement Biddle, the Commissary General of Forage, sent the rare and well-liked luxury, tea, which at this time was selling for about twenty dollars a pound. It is a matter of interest that the first public recognition of Washington's birthday occurred amid the cold and suffering at Valley Forge and came from the men in the ranks. Procter's Fourth Continental Artillery Band serenaded Headquarters that day, and Washington's appreciation of the compliment is recorded in the gratuity distributed to the bandsmen on February 27th. Four years later, in Rhode Island, Comte de Rochambeau, Commander-in-Chief of the French troops in America, gave to the day its first recognition as a public holiday by ordering a cessation of all labor by the French troops on February 12th, as February 11th, Washington's birthday, fell upon Sunday in 1781. Washington was born February 11, 1732, but the adoption of the Gregorian calendar by Great Britain in 1752 brought about a readjustment of dates so that his birthday ever since has fallen on February 22d.

Carrots, "pasnips," and cheese came as refreshing additions to the menu in March, and the practice of sending a man into the country to buy supplies for Headquarters every week or ten days was inaugurated. Mrs. Washington's thrift appears in the purchase of a crock for the butter the middle of this month, when the supply situation in general began to show signs of improvement. The tastes of the Commander-in-Chief were known to his friends, and the end of March, Lord Stirling sent him the first oysters of the season. The drink problem at Headquarters was more or less settled in March by the arrival of the first barrels of cider and home-brewed beer. Washington cared little for whiskey, rum, or strong, distilled liquors which were generally eschewed by the gentry of the day; but he had a discriminating taste for wine and claret. From March to June at Valley Forge seven barrels of beer and three barrels of cider were purchased for Headquarters. Milk was scarce, coffee there was none, and tea, at twenty dollars a pound and over, was not in abundance. By April the food situation had so improved as to be beyond the point of bother, and apples, parsnips, carrots, cabbages, and onions were obtainable in fair quantities.

The food situation in the winter of 1777–78 was somewhat parallel to the food situation to-day. The quantity in the country at large was more than sufficient; the trouble lay in the transportation, the depreciated currency, and large number of Tories in Pennsylvania and New Jersey. The proportion of the population of the Thirteen Original Colonies who were Loyalists during the Revolutionary War is not realized as generally as it should be. Our school his-

tories have carelessly or intentionally ignored the
facts, for the preponderance of the patriot feeling was
not so great as we have been led to believe. It is
doubtful if a referendum in all the Colonies on the
question of independence, during the winter of
1777–78 would have shown a healthy majority in its
favor.

The first sign of spring at Valley Forge is found in
the purchase, on April 10th, of a "mess of sprouts"
and a dozen shad. Mrs. Washington's preparations to
plunge into preserving are seen in the entries for the
purchase of nutmegs, "peper" and allspice, and soon
afterward, a sugar-loaf weighing one hundred and
twenty-one and one half pounds was procured at the
astounding cost of £91 2s. 6d. On the 18th of April
fifteen shad were purchased and "1 mess of sallard,"
two large tea-pots, four pounds of green tea, which
then cost nine pounds, and a bottle of snuff for twenty-
five shillings. Such entries as these lend a colorful
touch of intimacy to the record, and it is interesting to
see that Washington was akin to all dwellers of the
Potomac River basin in his taste for shad and oysters.
His liking for salad is beyond question, for, from April
until the army moved from Valley Forge, the purchases of salad and greens are too numerous to be
explained in any other way. The middle of May
7s. 6d. of "horse reddish" was purchased and the
welcome new delicacy of spring lamb arrived. Fish
was a favorite food, and the purchases of available

kinds were numerous. Twice, in June, presents of strawberries were sent to Headquarters, one from a Mrs. Henry, who lived near Valley Forge, and one from Mr. Mitchell, of Potts Grove.

An element of humor lurks in the charge of a gratuity of £3 15s. paid for the detection of a thief whose bibulous tastes succumbed to the temptations of the beer and cider barrels at Headquarters. A reward of about ten dollars for this detective work seems to imply that the thefts were of some consequence and rather cleverly managed. In contrast to this is the grim note of the not generally known execution of Thomas Shanks, a former ensign in the Tenth Pennsylvania Regiment, who was hanged as a spy near the Grand Parade at guard-mount on the 3d of June.

Preparations for the campaign of 1778 appear in the accounts about the middle of April. Two pairs of spur-leathers and two saddle girths were purchased for the General and his spurs carefully mended. Two new black stocks cost £6 5s. (about $16.50), and three dozen and two large gilt buttons and three dozen small ones cost £9 6s. 8d. The middle of May saw a general overhauling and mending of all the saddlery by Jeremiah Low, a saddler belonging to the Commander-in-Chief's Guard.

June 18, 1778, the British Army evacuated Philadelphia and started on its march across Jersey to New York City. The Continentals hastily broke camp and started in pursuit that same day, and the last entry of

expense at Valley Forge, as the Headquarters passed
into history, is the record of payment to Deborah
Hewes, of one hundred pounds Pennsylvania currency, "in full of all demands ag^t. his Excellency
Genl. Washington, for the use of her house & furniture
at V. Forge as pr. bill."

VII

THE COMMITTEES OF CORRESPONDENCE AND SAFETY OF THE REVOLUTIONARY WAR

THE development of the mechanics of a civil government to meet the necessities created by the struggle for political liberty is the most interesting of all the interesting phases of the American Revolution. In this development the Committees of Correspondence, of Observation, of Inspection, of Intelligence, and of Safety were most important organisms. They formed the bridge by which the colonists passed over the morass of political destruction from the ruins of a repudiated, paternalistic tyranny to the firm ground of self-administered government beyond.

"Prudence, indeed, will dictate that governments, long established, should not be changed for light and transient causes," wrote Jefferson, in the Declaration of Independence, but "whenever any form of government becomes destructive of these ends-[life, liberty, and the pursuit of happiness], it is the right of the people to alter or abolish it, and to institute new government, laying its foundation on such principles, and organizing its powers in such form, as to them shall seem most likely to effect their safety and happiness."

Accustomed to the obligation of meeting the difficult and oftentimes harsh demands of frontier life;

practiced in devising means of handling unusual situations, the colonists, as naturally as they built and assembled in their blockhouse forts to repel the Indian attack, rallied in communal groups to resist the aggressions of the Mother Country. Hampered in their legislatures by the dominating power of the royal governor, who by mere fiat checked or nullified the actions of the provincial assemblies and, when he saw fit, prorogued or dissolved them, the colonists, with the natural confidence of self-reliant men, were not long in devising a substitute for their thwarted legislative powers. The New England town meeting had early trained its hundreds to an understanding of community action, and the South was not inept in managing its own domestic affairs. The committee system was not an untried device in the Colonies, the assemblies had had experience in dealing with civic management through committee formation, and, in blocking the legal, natural channels of protest and remonstrance, the royal governors and other crown officers virtually instigated coöperative protest: committees of protesters were the result.

After the French and Indian War the trade discomfort caused by the so-called Sugar and Navigation Acts of the British Parliament led to the formation of committees of merchants in Massachusetts, Rhode Island, and New York. Through correspondence these committees planned a uniform method of protest and opposition by memorials to the provincial assemblies and by sending special representatives to England to remonstrate against these acts. Thus early the lesson was being learned that unity of protest is more effective than unrelated objections. But the results of these early efforts were disappointing. The General Court of Massachusetts, as that legislature was called, then appointed a committee of five, of which James Otis was chairman, to continue the opposition· to the Sugar Act during the recess of the Court, to write to the other Colonies, to inform them of the measures taken by Massachusetts to obtain the repeal of the act and to prevent the passage of the then pending Stamp Act. Unity of resistance is ever bred by usurpation and aggression that menaces or injures impartially and the other Colonies were asked to join with Massachusetts in adopting similar measures.

To establish a political machine of this character, extraneous to and unrecognized by any legal sanction, was difficult and dangerous as well. So dangerous was this that the Boston committee felt it wise to bind its members by oath not to divulge its proceedings. The towns of Massachusetts followed Boston's example and recommendation and the committee organization in that Colony gradually developed strength and efficiency. These committee efforts, the protests of the Stamp Act Congress, and the support of friends of America in England proved successful; the hated Stamp Act was repealed and the committees then gradually disintegrated, as there appeared to be no further need of effort. Only in Massachusetts were the organizations kept up.

The increasing pressure upon the Colonies was irksome, but the irritations appeared to rest unevenly, and it was not until the exasperated Rhode Islanders wreaked their vengeance upon His Majesty's revenue schooner *Gaspée*, by burning her to the water's edge, that the need of a united protest against despotic power was made clear. The royal instructions sent from Britain were to find, seize, and transport to England for trial the men who had burnt the *Gaspée*. The outburst of rage that greeted these instructions, when they became known, was more universal than any that had occurred in the Colonies before. The sacred right of trial by a jury of peers was here overridden by the king's ministers. It mattered not that no single culprit had been captured; the intent was there, plain to be read by every reading man, and the colonists were both reading and thinking men. The *Gaspée* offenders were known to every patriot in Providence, and, though not a single name was ever revealed to the crown officers, Rhode Island felt the menace of this display of arbitrary power and turned to Samuel Adams, of Massachusetts, for advice. His advice was sound. Send, said he, a circular letter to every one of the Colonies and ask for assistance. Rhode Island took this advice and issued a call for aid. It came as the rising tide and as irresistibly.

Under the conviction that all the Colonies must come to a common understanding as to the British claims to authority over them, which were a common menace to all and must be met by unity of action, the Virginia House of Burgesses resolved that a communication of sentiments between all the Colonies was necessary and that a standing Committee of Correspondence and Inquiry be appointed. This committee was to obtain the earliest authentic intelligence of all acts and resolutions of the British Parliament or administration which might affect America; it was to open and maintain a correspondence with all the other Colonies respecting these matters and to lay this correspondence and its proceedings thereon before the House of Burgesses from time to time. The committee was to inquire particularly into the constitutional authority and principles by which inhabitants of Rhode Island were to be transported beyond the seas for trial and the Speaker of the House was to transmit copies of these resolutions to the different assemblies and to request those assemblies to communicate, from time to time, with the Virginia Committee. When the Governor of Virginia learned of these resolutions, he promptly dissolved the House, but the members reconvened at a tavern and agreed upon a circular letter which Peyton Randolph, the Speaker of the House, was to send, with the resolves, to the different colonies as planned.

This bold questioning of Britain's authority met

with most enthusiastic support; Virginia's ringing call to action echoed up and down the Atlantic coast and before two months had passed the New England Colonies were solidly organized into committee groups, with rumors of like activity coming in steadily from the southward. The Royal Commission investigating the burning of the *Gaspée* thought it prudent to pause. The gathering storm-clouds appeared more ominous than the destruction of a dozen *Gaspées* and the Commissioners hastened to render an innocuous report that concerned itself more with the conduct of the commander of the *Gaspée* than with that of the unknown men who had destroyed her. No one was seized, no one was brought to trial, and the formidable ministerial attempt to punish, by overriding justice and right, ended in complete failure; and more than failure, for it accomplished for the Colonies what they had not been able to accomplish for themselves.

The Virginia resolves of March 12, 1773, were the signal for an intercolonial unity of action never before obtained. Before a year had passed, every Colony, except Pennsylvania, responded with a committee organization. Rhode Island, New Hampshire, Connecticut, and Massachusetts formed committees in May, 1773; South Carolina, in July; Georgia, in September; Maryland and Delaware, in October; North Carolina, in December; New York, in January, 1774; and New Jersey, in February.

That the movement, once launched, swept onward,

though the specific reason for it had disappeared, is evidence that the colonists were looking to the principles at stake rather than at any individual case of aggression. It was this group organization that controlled at the outbreak of the hostilities of the Revolutionary War, and it held steady the reins of governmental power and authority until the royalist machinery was shaken loose and democratic governments set up and set in motion. In the rosters of these committeemen of 1773 are to be found the names of nearly every Revolutionary patriot most familiar to us. The Massachusetts' list shows three signers of the Declaration of Independence, a delegate to the Continental Congress, and a major-general of the Continental Army; Rhode Island's a signer and two delegates to the Congress; Connecticut's a major-general, a commissary-general, and a commissioner to France; Maryland's two signers and three delegates to the Congress; Delaware's three signers; North Carolina's two and Virginia's seven signers, one of whom was the author of the Declaration itself.

In the natural and justifiable exultation over their victory, the colonists again relaxed their efforts to some extent, and Governor Thomas Hutchinson, of Massachusetts, wrote to the home Government in 1773 that:

I had the fullest evidence of a plan to engage the colonies in a confederation against the authority of Parliament. The towns of this province were to begin; the assembly to confirm their doings and to invite the other colonies to join.

The so-called Tea Act and Declaratory Act were next enacted by a Parliament intent upon enforcing entire submission to its will and, hard upon their heels, the Boston Tea Party flaunted its defiant opposition in the face of the royal Government just as the burning of the *Gaspée* had flashed the selfsame warning a year before. But the *Gaspée* was merely a mob assault upon an unpopular policeman; the Tea Party was open defiance of the law itself. The punishment was swift and drastic! The Boston Port Bill closed the harbor of Boston to all commerce; a British squadron blockaded the port and British regiments were landed in the town. Immediately the committee organization commenced to demonstrate its value. The Boston Committee held conference with those of the neighboring towns and addressed a circular letter to all the Colonies. The armed pressure imposed upon Boston was a fatal misstep. The Committees worked feverishly and the First Continental Congress was the result.

Up to the time of the calling of this Congress the Committees had been those of Correspondence, of Observation, of Inspection, and of Intelligence, or a combination of these titles such as Intelligence and Observation, of Correspondence and Inspection, or of Correspondence, Intelligence, and Inspection. Their functions were to write to the other Colonies; report conditions; keep watch over the non-importation resolutions and see to the punishment of violations; discuss and initiate protests and remonstrances to be forwarded to Parliament through the Colonial Agents in London, where such action, through the provincial assemblies, was blocked by the royal governors. By 1774 a new type of committee was coming into existence; that of the Committee of Safety. This committee rapidly became the most important of all. The titles now changed again, and there were Committees of Safety and Correspondence, of Safety and Observation, of Safety and Inspection; but in all the combinations the word "safety" took precedence. There was something ominous in the appearance of this word. It seemed to assume that the danger of a resort to force of arms might not be far distant.

The method of forming these committees was not always uniform in the different Colonies. The central or main Committee of Correspondence of the Colony was generally elected by the provincial assembly; the town and county committees by open convention of freeholders and inhabitants; these local committees, in turn, sometimes elected delegates from their membership to the main or central committee. In most cases, however, the central Committee of Correspondence of the province was chosen by the assembly and the personnel of the Committees of Safety well-nigh universally so. As they were to act for the assembly, when prorogued, or between sessions, the membership was invariably taken from that of the assembly itself. For this reason and also because the tenure of office of the committee was limited to the interim when there was no legislature, there was never any conflict of power or question of authority between the Committees of Safety and the legislatures.

Of the twelve Colonies represented in the First Continental Congress, four of them — Connecticut, New York, New Jersey, and Maryland — chose their delegates through their Committees of Correspondence; in one — Delaware — the delegates were chosen by a convention of inhabitants, called by the committees, and all the rest were either elected or appointed by the legislatures or at a general meeting of the inhabitants.

This First Continental Congress met in Philadelphia, September 5, 1774, and its non-importation resolution, adopted September 22, 1774, drew forth opposition which is of value to an understanding of the committees' work. Certain anonymous publications, entitled "Free Thoughts of a Westchester Farmer," asked:

Will you submit to this slavish regulation? You must. Our sovereign lords and masters the high and mighty delegates in Grand Continental Congress assembled, have ordered and directed it! They have directed the committees in the respective colonies to establish such further regulations as they may think proper for carrying the Association . . . into execution. If you like it better, choose your committee or suffer it to be chosen by half a dozen fools in your neighborhood; opening your doors to them — let them examine your tea canisters and molasses jugs, and your wives' and daughters' petticoats — bow and cringe and tremble and quake — fall down and worship our sovereign Lord, the Mob!

This was the production of the rector of Saint Peter's Episcopal Church in Westchester County, New York. He declared he would not submit to any such domination, and if "any pragmatical committee gentleman come to my house and give himself airs, I will show him the door, and if he does not soon take himself away, a good hickory cudgel shall teach him better manners." This excited author, the Reverend Mr. Samuel Seabury, was shocked and horrified at a people taking matters into its own hands. The Declaration of Independence had not then been written and he could not, evidently, conceive of the principle, laid down therein by Jefferson, that "the legislative powers, incapable of annihilation, have returned to the people at large, for their exercise." And their exercise, in Massachusetts, where the Ministerial troops held the provincial capital by the throat, was directed in a fashion succinctly displayed by the printed circular letter sent out from the Boston Committee of Correspondence to the committees of the near-by towns. February 25, 1775, two months before the battle of Lexington:

The following proceedings and votes of the joint Committees of this and several other towns are conveyed to you by their unanimous request. The importance of the subject at this critical time when our enemies are aided by some of our deluded fellow-citizens must strike you forcibly. We do not doubt but you will adopt the following or some similar plan as your salvation depends upon it. What you must do must be done soon, or it will be ineffectual. The army [British in Boston] by the number of wagons which they have engaged must be in want of a number of horses and cattle, it is wholly with our friends in the country to prevent their supply, but we need not dictate to them the mode. The cannon and baggage of the army must remain here unless you supply them with horses and cattle, but on your firmness and resolution we depend. We have a good cause, the thought is animating, take courage, and rely upon a kind Providence for protection and success in your resistance, in case it becomes necessary by your being attacked.

This was signed by William Cooper, Clerk of the Committee. Below it was printed the proceedings of the meeting referred to:

At a meeting of the Committees of Correspondence of the several towns of Boston, Charleston, Cambridge, Medford, Lexington, Watertown, Brookline and Concord —

Whereas the representative body of this Province in Congress, in Cambridge, considering that certain persons were employed in diverse kinds of work for the army, in order to enable it to take the field and distress the inhabitants of the country, did strongly recommend to the Committees of Correspondence and Inspection in the several towns and districts in this province, to see their resolves of the 7th instant, relative to supplying the troops now stationed in Boston, with timber, boards, spars, pickets, tent poles, canvas, bricks, iron, wagons, carts, carriages, intrenching tools or any materials for making any of the carriages or implements aforesaid, strictly and faithfully adhered to.

In compliance with the above recommendation and from a conviction of its being our duty to prevent such supplies. Voted, That the following methods, if strictly adhered to will, in our opinion, be effectual, *viz.* That no teams be suffered to load in, or after loading to pass through, any town in this province for Boston, if their load in whole or part, consists of any of the above mentioned articles, or oats, except the teamster can produce from the Committee of Correspondence for the town, where he loaded, an instrument, certifying his name, place of abode, the particulars of his load, the person who sends, and to whom to be delivered in Boston, and that said certificate ought to be delivered to one or more of the Committee of Correspondence for Boston before the teamster presumes to unload.

It is impossible to withhold admiration from action such as this. It was sabotage; but sabotage boldly and publicly recommended in the face of the bayonet.

The memorials, petitions, and addresses to the King, Parliament, and the people of Great Britain, of this First Continental Congress went for naught, and the Second Continental Congress assembled in Philadelphia a few weeks after the first shots of the war had been fired at Lexington. It recommended, on July 18th, to the various Colonies that each one appoint a committee of safety to superintend and direct all matters necessary for the security and defense of their respective Colonies in the recess of their assemblies and conventions. This was placing the seal of approval of the United Colonies upon the Committee of Safety system. Hostilities had begun, and a war de-

mands continuous and sustained effort that cannot
wait upon the established routine of peace-time custom. Early in 1775, Joseph Galloway, of Pennsylvania, came forward in his "Candid Examination of
the Mutual Claims of Great Britain and the Colonies" and paid his respects to the committee system
with the bitterness of excited toryism. He labeled the
Congress illegal and called upon the people to dissolve
their inferior committees — their instrument to tram-
ple on the sacred laws of their country and its invalu-
able rights. It was plainly evident to Galloway that
the committees were engines of power and accomplishment sufficient in themselves to overturn the
royal Government in the Colonies. The fact that
these committees were working in harmony with the
regular provincial legislatures, and that no conflict or
question of authority had developed made the matter, from the Loyalist viewpoint, most serious. He did
not see that because there was no conflict, because
there was no question of authority, the movement
possessed the greatest of all sanctions, that of unity of
purpose of an entire people. The royal governor could
muzzle or dissolve the legislature at will, whenever it
appeared to him that it was becoming too independent and unyielding in its antagonism to the measures
of the home Government; yet here was an organization, in which were to be found the most influential
men of the Colonies, which could not be reached or
controlled by any royal officer or crown power and

through which the legislature, though securely fet-
tered by the established royal practice, continued to
function freely in its rebellious attitude. It was both
disconcerting and alarming.

The central Committees of Safety became, from
their composition and character, the most important
and powerful of all the committees. During the tran-
sition period before the royal Government fell to
pieces and before the Revolutionary legislatures could
begin to function, they held, for a time, almost dicta-
torial power. But it was always wisely used and quietly wielded in coöperation with the local town and
county committees. Together these committees held
firm to the heavy, everyday work of massing the resources of the country behind the fighting forces. It
was not spectacular work, but exacting and unceas-
ing. A break in the lines of supplies, a check or delay
of men or equipment, a need for wagons, for arms, for
blankets for animals and fodder, and the Committee
of Safety was appealed to for aid. It called out the
militia, collected arms and accouterments, handled
desertions, received, managed, and guarded prisoners
of war, arrested Tories, adjusted accounts, settled
claims, and performed hundreds of other tasks of a
minor nature, but none the less necessary, which, un-
attended to, would have increased immeasurably the
burdens and difficulties of the war. Yet, important as
were these committees and this committee system,
after the advent upon the scene of the Committee of

In Committee of Safety

Philadelphia November 8th 1775

Gent.n

We have considered your respectful answer to our
application for the public arms in the County of Lancaster, and
are fully satisfied with the reasons you assign for retaining
them for the use of the poor Associators in said County, and have
only to acknowledge your Zeal in the Public Cause and to desire
you will send to us, the names of the persons in whose hands
the Arms are left, that it may be known where to apply for them
in any Emergency, and that public property may be taken
care of—

We also acknowledge your care in carrying
our Resolves, respecting Kearsley & Brooks into execution, and
we are, Gentlemen

Your most obedient
humble Servants—

To the Committee of Lancaster County

Signed by Order of the Board

B Franklin Presd.

Safety the career of all became comparatively brief. Few of them continued in existence beyond the year 1777. Only the New Hampshire and Connecticut Committees continued throughout the war; the Vermont, New York, and New Jersey Committees continued to 1778, and Rhode Island's lasted until 1781. All the others ceased functioning as soon as the Revolutionary legislatures took firm control of affairs; this was usually as soon after the Declaration of Independence as the different States could adopt new constitutions and put them into operation. The Committees of Correspondence had virtually merged with the Committees of Safety after the war commenced, and the entire committee organization, as a part of the Revolutionary War machine, had dissolved by January, 1778. A good picture of the way in which the committees functioned is furnished in the letter from the Commander-in-Chief to the New York Committee, July 22, 1777:

GENTLEMEN,

I am informed by General George Clinton that you have vested him with powers to call out the Militia of the Counties of Ulster, Orange, Dutchess and Westchester until the 1st August, at which time the New Legislature of the State is summoned to meet. As it will probably be some time before the wheels of the New Government can be put in motion, I am fearful, that unless this Power is extended to a further time, there will be a vacancy between Genl. Clinton's present Commission, and the enacting new Laws by the Legislature, a circumstance, which at this time may prove most fatal in its consequences, because from the present appearance of matters, the enemy are upon the point of making some capital move. I would therefore wish, if it can be done with propriety, that before your Board is dissolved, you would extend this power of calling out the militia to Genl. Clinton, or some other person, till such time as you may reasonably expect the New Legislature will have met and proceeded regularly to business.

I mention Genl. Clinton or some other person, because as he will enter into his office of Governor of the State upon the 1st of August, he cannot probably attend to the Business of calling out the Militia. If you are of opinion that he can, I would prefer him to any other.

I have the honor to be, Gentlemen,
Your Most Obdt. and Humbl. Servt.
Go. Washington.

In studying the history of our Revolutionary War, it is but natural that our attention should first be caught by the high lights and brilliant color of the exciting events of the military conflict, or the romance of the diplomatic scenes, to the exclusion of the commonplace, everyday efforts of the average citizen; but a closer study of such phases of that struggle as this committee organization suggests will well repay the effort involved. For here and elsewhere we shall find, in the picture that unrolls before our eyes, the practical workings of a democracy at its best, which holds for all of us the inspiration that is so valuable a part of our great heritage from the American Revolution.

VIII

THE CONTINENTAL ARMY UNIFORM

THE uniform of the Continental Army was a costume of growth, governed largely by sectional taste and the difficulty of obtaining supplies. During the Revolution clothing was a primal necessity; style, color, and trimmings were secondary. The war was half over before there was an appreciable result from the efforts to establish a definite Continental Army uniform, if indeed there could be said to have been a consistent effort on the part of any central authority to establish such a uniform. After one attempt in November, 1775, Congress did not undertake to concern itself with the uniform problem beyond the matter of obtaining the cloth and clothing. Washington was alive to the advantages of an established uniform, but hesitated to issue orders that would involve the scantily paid officers and the Continentals in extra and avoidable expense. The sparsely settled and loosely organized Colonies were unequal to the strain of suddenly furnishing an army of several thousand men with a uniform costume in which color and specialties of decoration played an important part and where dependence was, perforce, largely placed upon importations from Europe.

The blue and buff that instinctively comes to mind

whenever we think of the Continental soldier is a curious survival of mixed impressions, helped out by the costume portraits and Revolutionary paintings of Trumbull, Peale, and others of less fame. The blue is certainly right, for before the war was over that color had become the recognized ground of the Continental coat; but authority for the buff is lacking. Probably the firmest basis for this, as for everything else that is military in Revolutionary War history, rests in the natural thought of George Washington. Blue and buff was the uniform of the First Virginia Regiment commanded by Colonel George Washington in the French and Indian War; blue and buff was the uniform he wore the day that Dr. Thatcher first saw him at Cambridge and described him for us in his well-known diary, and blue and buff was the uniform coat of the Commander-in-Chief's Guard which was formed March 12, 1776.

It is not possible to give positively the reason for the selection of blue. A number of ingenious explanations have been advanced, one of them going back through the Cromwellian Wars even to Biblical authority; but perhaps as good a guess as any is that we find blue predominating as a colonial uniform color in King George's and the French and Indian Wars, because the King's regulars frowned upon, if they did not actually forbid the provincials to adopt the sacred red coat of the British grenadier. What more natural, then, as a distinctive color was wanted and red could not be used, than to think of the counterpart, blue?

The necessity of a uniform for the fighting men has been obvious from the time of the first group conflicts. The practical reasons, first of distinguishing friends from enemies, is probably basic; though intimidating the enemy by ferocity of costume was a factor. Old Chinese and Japanese armor demonstrate this idea, and Washington's order of July 24, 1776, shows its survival to that time. A moral support also is drawn from the association of large numbers of men all clad alike and a stiffening of personal esteem, which is manufactured courage, results from a costume, handsome and decorative in the eyes of the individual wearing it.

Though the Revolutionary War was several years old before the fruits of the efforts made to bring the Continental Army into a uniform garb became perceptible, yet they were slow of the desired effect only because of the scarcity of materials and not because the advantages of uniformity were unthought of or disregarded.

The earliest mention of uniform insignia in the Washington Papers is found in a little leather-covered account book of personal expenses for 1775, where an entry for July 10th stands: "By Ribbon to distinguish myself......3/4." This ribbon was a broad one of light blue color which was worn diagonally across Washington's chest, between his coat and waistcoat.

The various States that sent their troops to Cambridge to aid in the siege of Boston sent them clad in all the variegated uniforms that had pleased the taste of the militia train bands. Few State regulations specifying a uniform for the State militia can be found, and, of the Thirteen Colonies, only New York and New Jersey appear to have hit upon the blue and buff combination for their troops. Quite a number of the independent organizations used blue as a ground color with scarlet, white, or green facings; but gray, brown, and red coats with varied facings, some buff, were not unusual.

Before Washington had been in command a week, the lack of distinctive uniforms had interfered with the duties of the general officers in an embarrassing and irritating manner. Under orders the sentries stopped all whom they did not know from passing the lines at the outposts, and when, on such occasions, the officer of the guard was summoned, it frequently happened that he, too, did not know the generals. How often this happened to the Commander-in-Chief himself we do not know, but on July 10th, Washington purchased the light blue ribbon, and on July 14th issued a general order that the Commander-in-Chief would be distinguished by this "ribband wore across his breast, between his coat and waistcoat. The Majors and Brigadiers-General by a pink ribband wore in like manner and the Aids de Camp by a green ribband." Later it seemed proper to distinguish the major-generals from the brigadiers, so their ribbon was changed to purple.

July 13th the general orders had commented upon the inconvenience of the unfortunate situation of the Continental Army in not having uniforms, and had endeavored to bring about a clearer understanding and stricter discipline by suggesting that the field officers wear red or pink cockades in their hats, the captains yellow or buff, and the subalterns green. The officers were ordered to furnish themselves accordingly. The non-commissioned officers were to be distinguished by an epaulet or stripe of red cloth on the right shoulder and the corporals by one of green. Though these orders fixed matters temporarily for the recognition of the officers, the uniform of the private soldier was still undetermined, and the inconvenience of this was voiced in Colonel Loammi Baldwin's letter to Washington of August 16, 1775, in which he states that he "should be much obliged to your Honour if you could send me word who settles the uniforms for the several regiments that compose the American Army & whether they are numbered yet."

The question of uniform clothing was considered among other important matters by a committee of several delegates to the Continental Congress and the Governors of Connecticut, Rhode Island, Massachusetts, and New Hampshire, which conferred with Washington at Headquarters, the latter part of October, 1775. The committee recommended that the cloth from which the uniforms were to be made be dyed brown and that the regimental distinctions be made in the facings. It was further recommended that the soldiers pay for their own clothing by means of stoppages of one and two thirds dollars a month out of their meager pay of six and two thirds dollars. Congress adopted both of these recommendations on October 23d, so that the official uniform color first adopted for the Continental Army was brown.

Apparently there was some delay in settling the regimental facing distinctions, for by the middle of November the colonels of the newly established army were directed by general orders of the 23d to settle with the Quartermaster-General as soon as possible the uniform of their respective regiments, that the buttons might be properly numbered and no delay experienced for want of these necessary findings. The buttons were made of pewter, stamped with the number of the regiment, and some few of them are still in existence; later they were cloth-covered in the proper colors. Another difficulty experienced was the attempts of the soldiers to eke out their small pay by selling their clothing, so a strict order was issued November 19th, against any one buying clothing from soldiers under pain of being made a military prisoner and so deprived of the processes of civil law. The last of the year an attempt was made to obtain uniformity of clothing by the general order of December 11th, in which Washington

earnestly recommended to the officers to put themselves in a proper uniform. The Field Officers of each of the new Corps will set the example by clothing themselves in the Regimentals of their respective Corps. . . . the General by no means recommends or desires officers to run into costly or expensive Regimentals; no matter how plain or coarse they are so they are but uniforms in their Coulour, Cut and Fashion. The officers belonging to those regiments whose uniforms are not yet fixed upon had better delay making their regimentals until they are.

There was no thought of the visibility of the uniform in Revolutionary times, for with the comparatively short range of the musket, rifle, and artillery fire, the combatants needed to be so near each other that little concealment was possible.

The Commander-in-Chief's Guard was formed by general orders of March 12, 1776, and the uniform selected for them was the blue coat and buff facings of the old First Virginia Colonial Regiment. The waistcoat was red, the breeches of buckskin, and the hat of black felt, bound with white tape; the cross-belts, stockings, and gaiters were white. In the middle of the year 1776 the difficulty of obtaining clothing is well pictured by Washington's general order of July 24th, which stated that the General,

being sensible of the difficulty and expense of providing cloaths of almost any kind for the troops, felt an unwillingness to recommend, much less to order, any kind of uniform, but as it is absolutely necessary that men should have Cloaths and appear decent and tight, he earnestly encourages the use of hunting shirts with long breeches made of the same cloth, gaiter fashion about the legs, to all those yet unprovided. No dress can be cheaper, nor more convenient, as the wearer may be cool in warm weather and warm in cool by putting on under-cloaths which will not change the outward dress, Winter or Summer — Besides which it is a dress justly supposed to carry no small terror to the enemy, who think every such person a complete marksman.

Here is the survival of the practice of intimidating the enemy by means of costume, and the order marks the adoption of the long trouser idea in the United States Army. It was due to the deadly accuracy of the fire of Colonel Daniel Morgan's Virginia Rifle Regiment, that the white linen hunting-shirt, with its fringed skirt, cape, and trousers was an object the British trooper disliked to see before him. After witnessing the havoc wrought by the long-barreled rifles of the Virginia hunters, General Burgoyne is reported to have said to Colonel Morgan at the surrender of Saratoga: "My dear Sir, you command the finest body of men in the world."

In October, the Continental Congress passed a resolution designed to encourage enlistments by offering a clothing bounty to those men who would enlist for the entire period of the war. The extra allowance to non-commissioned officers and privates consisted of a yearly grant of two linen hunting-shirts, two pairs of overalls, one leather or woolen waistcoat, one pair of breeches, one hat or leather cap, two shirts, two pairs of shoes, and one pair of hose. The value of all this was twenty dollars.

A year later a regimental coat was added with additional breeches, stockings, and a blanket which was supposed to bring the total value up to fifty-six dollars. Up to the year of 1777, the clothing supplies for the army were largely obtained through importation and privateer captures; but in March of that year James Mease was appointed Clothier-General to the army by Washington, under authority of the resolve of Congress of December 27, 1776; and in the instructions given him to put the clothing supply on a sound basis, Washington suggested that he lay before Congress "an estimate of the clothing necessary for the next campaign with the colors of the clothes proper to put the troops into distinct uniforms, which is a thing that cannot possibly be done this year." The Continental regiments in many cases had already fixed upon a uniform for themselves, and the most economical course was to continue the selected uniform when issuing clothing to these regiments, which Mease was directed to do. Another of Washington's practical suggestions was to rip the lining out of the heavy woolen coats and make it up into waistcoats and drawers for the men in winter, the coats so lightened being that much cooler in the summer months.

Among the many difficulties of the uniform problem an unexpected and needless one obtruded itself in the rather foolish selection by Moylan's Continental Dragoons of a red uniform with blue facings. As soon as Washington heard of this, he objected strongly, as the combination was the same as that worn by the Queen's Dragoons of the British Army and he feared some fatal mistakes would result. Moylan's officers, however, had already fitted themselves out, and as Washington was unwilling to put them to the heavy expense of changing, the Clothier-General delivered to the corps two hundred and forty captured coats of the Twenty-First and Eighth British Foot, which were red, faced with blue. As the best way out of an awkward situation, Washington then directed that Colonel Moylan put linen frocks over the dragoon uniform whenever there was the slightest apparent need of guarding against mistakes. Cavalry could easily carry the extra garment. Before long, however, even this precaution proved insufficient, and a party of Moylan's dragoons came perilously close to being fired upon as they returned to camp, so Washington peremptorily ordered Moylan to dye his uniforms, any color, so long as it was not red.

Though Washington's preference was for the blue uniform, he did not object to the brown as he considered the brown and white and the brown and buff combinations "good standing colors." Uniforms of the Eighth, Twenty-First, Forty-Seventh, Fifty-Third and Sixty-Second British Foot were captured in sufficient quantities at Saratoga to clothe several Continental battalions, but the private soldiers objected to the red uniforms, though the quality of the cloth was unusually good and the officers were eager for them. The coats of the Sixty-Second Foot had buff facings and the Clothier-General did not think it worth while to change these, as the difference between buff and white was not very noticeable in a battalion. Washington's instructions to Mease in May, 1777, furnish us with a picture of the clothing situation of the army in 1776 and 1777. He urged the Clothier-General to lay his estimates for clothing for 1778 before the Secret Committee of Congress at once, "or next Spring all will be confusion again and the Army come into the field half clad in a thousand different colors as to uniform." A minor consideration seems to have been that if a man could be recognized by his corps uniform, he would be hindered from committing many faults for fear of detection.

There was some difficulty encountered in dyeing the British red coats from the high cost of the copperas needed and the labor and time involved. Unless the coats were ripped apart the dye did not penetrate the seams, which continued to show red lines, and the coats, as a whole, shrunk a little in size. If they were ripped apart, there were so many small pieces of cloth to handle that some of them were sure to be lost and the time involved in sewing the coats together again could not be spared. The difficulty was overcome in a measure by changing the cuffs, capes, and lapels, and it was Brigadier-General George Weedon's opinion that these changes made the coats readily distinguishable from the British uniform. The wide cross-belts over the chest and the front facing did obscure the coat's color so that practically only the sleeves showed the ground of the uniform from the front, and the virtue of necessity forced the compromise.

During the dark days of Valley Forge, Washington again attempted to improve the uniform situation by devising a new model of coat which, he wrote the Clothier-General, could be made quicker and cheaper, and yet be warmer and more convenient for the men. He would send a model of the new coat, he said, as soon as one could be made up, and gave it, as his opinion, that the whole army should be dressed in this fashion. There appears to be no record of what this new-fashioned coat was, and as the uniform for 1778 shows little, if any, variation in cut and trimming from those of 1776 and 1777, it was presumed that the usual obstacles of scarcity of material and want of time prevented the change.

After the decision of Congress on November 4, 1775, to dye the uniform cloth brown, there was no well-defined attempt to change from that color until October, 1778, when a supply of clothing arrived from France in which there were an almost equal number of blue and brown coats. A return of these uniforms shipped to Headquarters at Fredericksburg,

New York, between the 12th and 27th of October, 1778, shows that 4674 brown coats with red facings and 3613 blue coats with red facings, 8439 white waistcoats and 8343 white breeches, together with several thousand pairs of hose and shoes and over nine thousand blankets were in the shipment. Before they were received, it was known in camp that both blue and brown coats were in the shipment, and, to forestall disputes and to give all an equal chance, a lottery was held at Headquarters in which Robert Hanson Harrison drew for the North Carolina troops, Richard Kidder Meade for Virginia and Delaware, Tench Tilghman for Maryland, James McHenry for Pennsylvania, and Alexander Hamilton for New Jersey. All of these gentlemen were lieutenant-colonels and aides to the Commander-in-Chief. Captain Henry Philip Livingston, of the Commander-in-Chief's Guard, drew for New York; Major Caleb Gibbs, Commandant of the Guard, drew for Massachusetts; and Colonel Alexander Scammell, Adjutant-General of the Continental Army, drew for New Hampshire and Hazen's Canadian regiment. The colors thus drawn were blue for North Carolina, Maryland, New Jersey, and New York, and brown for Virginia, Delaware, Pennsylvania, Massachusetts, and New Hampshire and the Canadians. After this was settled, it seemed that there might possibly be some of the blue coats left after North Carolina and the other fortunate troops were supplied, so, to prevent ill feeling, a second lottery was held for those who had drawn brown coats on the first. This one was to settle the order of choice for the surplus blue coats until the supply was exhausted. In this drawing Massachusetts obtained first choice, Virginia and Delaware second, New Hampshire and Hazen's third, and Pennsylvania last.

These lotteries show plainly that by 1778 the preference of the man in the ranks was for blue coats. The complete record of these two lotteries is still preserved in the Washington Papers, and even the little squares of paper which were drawn are still in existence, marked and signed as drawn by the different officers.

By March, 1779, it was found necessary to put a stop to the practice which had grown up of regiments adopting such uniforms as their taste directed, for the resultant lack of regularity had proved so inconvenient and expensive that in the regulations that Congress adopted, March 23d, for the Clothing Department, the Commander-in-Chief was authorized and directed to fix and prescribe the uniform of the army, as well with regard to color and facings as the cut or fashion of the clothes to be worn by the troops of the respective States; but, owing to the difficulties of material and tailoring, the saving clause was inserted that the Commander-in-Chief's regulations were to be "as far as possible complied with by all purchasing agents, officers and soldiers according to the circumstances of supplies." Here plainly is the reason why the Continental Army as late as the fourth year of the war did not have a distinct official uniform. The scarcity of materials is still more plainly accented by Anthony Wayne's failure in September, 1779, to obtain a distinctive uniform for his cherished Light Infantry. Washington was in sympathy with his desire, but deemed it inadvisable, for as the Light Infantry was a corps made up by detail from the Continental Line, the men ought to wear the uniform of the regiments from which they were taken. The Commander-in-Chief considered that "though this from diversity is not favorable to their appearance, the contrary would be a deviation from the common practice and would not fail to create uneasiness. Besides," he naïvely argued, "whenever the men return to their regiments, the diversity of uniform would be more disagreeable." Evidently the clothing supply would not warrant an additional uniform for a separate service. Nearly a year later a concession was made to the Light Infantry in the shape of permission to wear black and red feathers in their hats, to distinguish the corps from the rest of the army, and all other officers and soldiers were forbidden to wear these colored feathers.

It was in response to the regulations of March 23d, that Washington issued his general order of October 2, 1779, establishing the uniform of the Continental Army and settled finally and for all time upon blue as the ground color; until supplanted by the khaki of the Spanish-American War, blue was the army color of the United States troops. The order of October 2d read:

The following are the uniforms that have been determined for the troops of these States respectively as soon as the State of the Public Supplies will permit their being furnished accordingly and in the meantime it is recommended to the Officers to endeavor to accommodate their Uniforms to the Standard that when the men come to be Supplied there may be a proper uniformity — *Artillery and Artillery Artificers:* Blue, faced with Scarlet, Scarlet lining, Yellow buttons, Yellow bound hats, Coats edged with narrow lace or tape & button holes bound with same. *Light Dragoons:* The Whole Blue, faced with White, White buttons and Linings. *N.H., Mass., R.I., Conn.:* Blue, faced with white, Buttons and lining white. *N.Y., N.J.:* Blue, faced with Buff, White linings and buttons. *Pa., Del., Md., Va.:* Blue, faced with Red, Buttons and linings White. *N.C., S.C., Ga.:* Blue, faced with Blue, Button holes edged with narrow white lace or tape, Buttons and linings white.

It was evident that this explicit settlement of the uniform question was only partially successful, for, nearly ten months later, on July 19, 1780, at Preakness, New Jersey, the general orders again called attention to the need of uniformity and ordered the officers not to change either their own uniform or that of their men until a general rule was decided upon. At the same time a touch of jauntiness was given to the uniforms of the major-generals by directing that

the feathers in their hats be of black and white, with
the black above and the white below. It was suggested that there be but one feather, with the upper
part dyed black. Other officers below the rank of
major-general were to have black and white cockades,
a black ground with a white relief which would be
emblematic of the approaching union of the American
and French armies.

Since March 23, 1779, when it turned the matter of
the uniform over to the Commander-in-Chief, Congress had paid no attention to it; but, on February 28,
1781, a resolution was passed reciting the wisdom of
discouraging extravagance and inculcating economy.
This wisdom, combined with a proper patriotism, de-
creed that after January 1, 1782, no officer in the
service should wear on his clothes any gold or silver
lace or vellum other than such as Congress or the
Commander-in-Chief of the Army or Navy should
direct for the uniform of the corps and badges to distinguish officers, or, that on or after that date, no
officer of any description in the Army or Navy of the
United States or any other officer in their service
should wear any uniform usually worn by the British
Army or Navy.

When Cornwallis surrendered at Yorktown, a quantity of British clothing fell into the hands of the Continentals, as had been the case at Saratoga, and the
Clothier-General's letter to Washington, December
27, 1781, shows that, even when there were coats to

distribute, the matter was not entirely simple. John
Moylan, then the Clothier-General, was at Newburgh watching a chance to get the clothing across
the frozen Hudson River from Fishkill Landing. He
wrote:

> The British coats have been for some time past all dyed
> and have received no damage in the colouring — enough
> still remains to complete the Connecticut Line, or the New
> York and New Jersey line *Jointly*, the former refuse taking
> them on account of the Colour, the only possible objection
> they have any grounds for. Were these coats delivered to
> either of the above I should have it in my power to clothe
> every line uniformly.

Just what was the result of this job of dyeing the
red uniforms with copperas is unrecorded, but it may
be assumed that as the Connecticut soldier failed to
approve, it could not have been quite the success that
the Clothier-General claimed.

The uniform coat of the Continental and British
armies and also of the French expeditionary force was
quite similar in cut and fashion. They were all snug-
fitting as to shoulders and waist, with skirts that
reached to the knee. The collar of the Continental
Army coat was sometimes straight standing with
broad lapels which at times widened out into a short
cape effect around the shoulders in imitation of the
hunting-shirt costume of the riflemen. A record of
exact dimensions and definite rules for making the
coat has survived in the report of a board of officers in
January, 1781, who considered the style of coat to be

adopted by the Massachusetts line. The color of the coat, waistcoat, buttons, and linings, as established in the general order of October 2, 1779, was adhered to, but the dimensions of the coat were exactly given. It was to be cut high in the neck, with the exact number of inches specified for lapel width and the holding button on the shoulder. The lapel was to begin at the waist and its wing to button one inch from the shoulder seam. This long lapel obviated the necessity of the front facing. The cuff was to be close, with four worked buttonholes; the pockets scalloped and with four buttonholes also. The exact number of buttons was specified. The bottom of the coat was cut square and the skirts turned back and fastened by a button or other device, to show the lining. The waistcoat was single-breasted and long, with flap pockets. Our present-day vest is, of course, but a shrunken waistcoat. Knee-breeches, with heavy woolen stockings, were first worn and the ankles were gaitered in varying heights with the same material as the breeches. These breeches were of buckskin, cloth, linen, and sometimes of canvas or sailcloth. Later the overall, or long trousers, were adopted as being cheaper and more practical in every way. Gaiters were worn with these or they were split and buttoned at the bottom close around the ankle. The coats were made of broadcloth and wool; the waistcoats of wool, buckskin, or any cloth obtainable, and the overalls, hunting-shirts, and gaiters, of linen, canvas, sailcloth, or osnaburgs, this latter a coarse cloth made of flax and tow. In 1780 the cost of the private soldier's uniform was twenty-four shillings, with those of the non-commissioned officers, drummers, and fifers a trifle more.

The hat of the Continental soldier was of felt or thick cloth, with a low crown and broad circular brim which was caught up and fastened to the crown at three equidistant points; the edges were sometimes bound with tape. The cockades, or rosettes, of the corps distinctions were fastened to one of these points and some little attention was necessary to keep the cockades of a company all on the same side of the head. A supply of hats in 1782 called forth a general order, on May 14th, for the regiments to cast lots for the first choice in sizes. The commanding officers were directed to be "extremely attentive to give the hats a military and uniform appearance by cutting, cocking or adding such other decorations as they think proper." This order also directed the Clothier-General to furnish, if possible, worsted shoulder knots for the non-commissioned officers. The sergeants were to wear knots on both shoulders, the corporals one on the right shoulder only. If the knots could not be obtained, a piece of white cloth was to be substituted by way of distinction. The hat-cocking was evidently a success, for it was commended in the orders of August 12th, and a uniform method of hair-tying suggested.

The end of the year 1782 saw the last change in the Continental uniform when Benjamin Lincoln, then Secretary of War, wrote to Washington on December 2d, and ordered that the coats in the future be faced with red and that they have white linings and buttons. Lincoln gave as the reason for this order that the change appeared to him to be wished for when he conversed with the officers at camp. In compliance with this, Washington issued the general order of December 6, 1782, that as the Secretary of War has been pleased to direct

that the uniform of the American Cavalry and Infantry shall in the future be a blue ground with red facings and white linings and buttons, the General gives this early notice that provision may be made accordingly before the Army shall receive their clothing for the present year. The Corps of Artillery is to retain its present uniform and the Sappers and Miners will have the same.

A scarcity of material, characterized as "inevitable circumstances," rendered it necessary to exempt the Light Infantry from this order, and on March 3, 1783, all Light Infantry companies were granted the privilege of blue coats with white facings until further orders, so that what the corps of Barren Hill, Stony Point, and Yorktown fame had so earnestly desired and richly deserved, came to it at last, through the very poverty that had denied it at first.

The scarcity of uniforms continued throughout the war and up to the very disbanding of the army. On

February 24, 1783, on account of the non-arrival of clothing the troops were ordered to turn their old coats of the preceding year, and were informed at the same time that scarlet cloth for cuffs, capes, and half facings would be supplied them. A month and a half passed and this order had been but partially obeyed, so a small bribe was offered in the shape of an extra allowance of one ration per coat for every regimental coat that had been or should be turned.

It thus appears that the uniform, in which the Continental Army started upon its long struggle for victory, was brown; that after the war was half over this color changed to blue with white linings and facings predominating; and that the war ended with the army in a blue uniform coat with red facings.

IX

BREAD AND THE SUPERINTENDENT OF BAKERS
OF THE CONTINENTAL ARMY

THE ration of a soldier is always a fixed quantity and
the amount of bread issued daily to the Continental
private was one pound. Circumstances varied this
amount slightly at different times during the Revolution, but the full quantity never rose above one and
one quarter pounds nor fell below three quarters of a
pound at any time that bread was obtainable. Ap-
proximately one pound of bread has always formed a
part of the daily ration of the American soldier since
the time of the Revolution.

Lexington and the siege of Boston brought an army
into existence almost overnight, and an army that
grew in numbers daily. Food for this suddenly concentrated body of men became a subsistence problem
that was met with varied skill by the train-band captains and higher officers. These were not men entirely
inexperienced in such matters, for King George's and
the old French and Indian War had taught the
colonial militiamen practical, if severe, lessons and,
though the military subsistence problems of 1775
were not easily solved, they were met with such intelligence that as long as the army remained stationary,
on the lines around Boston, the food supply was not a

matter of great difficulty. With the evacuation of the town by the British, and the commencement of the first march of the Continental Army from Boston to New York, came the first real test of the commissary department.

Bread was one of the three principal parts of the soldier's ration, and any reduction of the quantity, or an entire lack of supply, was more severely felt by the troops than a loss of beef, vegetables, or rum. Congress established the ration of the soldier as to quantity and variety, but made no provision for a system that would ensure a regular supply of the food authorized. Before the appointment of a superintendent of baking, the companies had obtained bread by selecting one of their number to bake bread for them and one or two other men were usually detailed as assistants. Flour was issued instead of bread and the men pooled their receipts and handed it to the comrade chosen to do the baking, or else, if they were in a thickly settled part of the country, the individual soldier traded in his loose flour to the country folk in return for bread, or dickered with the camp traders, who followed the army, for either bread or rum. This practice was uncertain and uneven in its results. In the first instance it permitted the company baker to make such a tidy profit (one pound of flour will make much more than one pound of bread and the baker kept the surplus as his perquisite) that there was an instance of one or two soldiers making so much profit, by baking for one of the artillery regiments (two hundred and fifty to three hundred men), that they were able to lend the commissary, in an emergency, one thousand rations of flour for eight days. These baking privates used as much water in the bread as they pleased, as there was no inspection, and sold the surplus flour to the country folk, or, if they were not satisfied with the price, loaded the flour in public wagons and transported it to a better market. The individual soldier, with flour trading as his excuse, straggled and plundered and roused the ire of the country people by his marauding practices.

The lack of system and the evil effects therefrom were not plainly evident at first, for, before the Continental Army had been six months in the field, the British arrived in New York Bay, and the battle and retreat from Long Island ensued. This was followed by a desperate campaign of fighting and retreat that left small time for considering any plans other than those of combat and flight. Forts Washington and Lee were lost, the retreat through the Jerseys followed, Trenton and Princeton were added to the immortal honor roll of the Continental Army, and the tired regiments were established in winter quarters at Morristown before a decided move could be made to put the bread supply upon a stable footing.

The army bread was almost entirely hard bread, what we now know as hard-tack or ship's biscuit. Soft bread was something of a luxury and does not seem to have been very highly esteemed by the men in the ranks. The ration of loose flour gave the soldier a chance to obtain rum, and, where he did not trade for anything but bread, he declined the soft variety as it was bulky to carry, if more than one day's rations were issued, easily spoiled and more apt to be sour and unwholesome than the hard variety, which, though made without salt or rising, was compact, easy to carry, and remained edible for days in any temperature. When conveniences were lacking, the men baked their own bread on stones, with far from satisfying results, and the satirical name among the soldiers for such bread was "fire cake."

It was not until the war was entering upon its third year, in May, 1777, that Congress took steps to ensure a proper supply of the staff of life to the army. The man selected for this important work was an old gingerbread baker in Philadelphia, who, at the call, gave up a well-paying business and a comfortable old age to share the hardships of military life with an army in the field and to make himself responsible for a most important part of that army's subsistence. Christopher Ludwick was fifty-seven years old when he accepted the appointment by the Continental Congress of "Superintendent of Bakers and Director of Baking in the Grand Army of the United States."

He was not unknown in Philadelphia, for he had been in the city, following his trade of baker, since the French and Indian War. He was not unknown to

Congress, for he had helped to forward a supply of powder to Ticonderoga in 1775 and, after the Trenton victory, he had taken charge of and fed some of the Hessian prisoners, and wrought so cannily with them that they succeeded in inducing the desertion of several of their brethren from within the British lines, who came over to the patriots bringing their arms and accouterments with them.

This appointment by Congress gave Ludwick power to license, with approval of the Commander-in-Chief, or the commanding officers of separate armies or posts, all persons to be employed in baking for the troops; to regulate their pay and take any necessary steps to rectify all the then existing difficulties and failures of the bread supply. He was given seventy-five dollars a month as pay and two rations per day. It is current tradition that when Ludwick's pay was discussed by the committee of Congress it was suggested that he be granted the perquisite of furnishing only eighty pounds of bread for every hundred pounds of flour and that the old man had replied with scorn: "Is it that I should grow rich by such ways? I will bake one hundred and thirty-five pounds of bread for every hundred pounds of flour, and it will be good bread and all the flour will be used, and if there is any flour over, it will also be made into bread."

The army was at Morristown when Ludwick left Philadelphia to take charge of the baking, and he had hardly time to do more than start operations before the campaign opened and the troops broke camp and moved out upon, what was to be, the most active marching campaign of the war. The peculiar uncertainty of movement displayed by the British commander-in-chief at the beginning of the campaign of 1777, was responsible for much of the marching and countermarching of the Continentals; the troops were almost daily on the move and an enormous supply of bread had to be ready, to meet the continual emergencies caused by unexpected changes in direction of the line of march. To add to these difficulties inexcusable losses of bread occurred from careless handling. Hundreds of pounds of crisp, browned bread would be sent from Ludwick's ovens to the troops in the field, and because no particular officer had been designated to receive it, it sometimes remained in the open, beside the camp, in the blazing heat of the day and the damp of the night dew. The commissaries of issues declared it was not their affair and the quartermaster officers declined the responsibility of issuing it to the troops, and old Ludwick stormed and swore great oaths at such official stupidity.

When the army turned south from the Highlands, General George Clinton ordered thirty thousand pounds of hard bread, which had been stored at Fort Montgomery, sent on to the marching troops by way of King's Ferry, and found that, for lack of proper storage, most of it was so badly broken it could not be transported and was unfit for use. He attempted to save the unbroken part by collecting casks in which to pack it; but none were to be had, so he sent a hurry call to the Continental storehouse at Fishkill to properly pack and forward thirty thousand pounds from there.

Ludwick's principal troubles were not in the baking of the bread, but in the arrangements necessary before the ovens could be charged and afterwards in getting the bread away to the troops. While he was in control there were but few complaints as to the quality of the bread issued. There was at first some difficulty in obtaining the flour for baking from the commissaries or storekeepers of the different divisions, or posts. Congress made no provision for paying the bakers which it authorized Ludwick to employ, and the old man used his private means to advance the pay of those of his bakers who were civilians; soldiers detailed from the ranks as helpers were on a different footing; but Ludwick kept them in humor by small gratuities. To accomplish this he sold several of his houses in Philadelphia and expended the tidy little fund of ready cash (£3500) that he had made from his gingerbread baking before the war. He paid these wages regularly every two months, and before he was reimbursed by the military paymasters, he suffered further losses through the depreciation of the Continental currency.

The difficulties of distribution of the bread after it was baked so worried the Superintendent of Bakers that he appealed to Congress to specially designate an officer for each group of troops, in barracks, or field, whose duty it should be to requisition for the bread and receive it from the ovens. This officer, Ludwick urged, should furnish covered wagons for the bread, wagons with tight, strong bodies and stout enough to hold a ton in weight. The army on the march spread over a large tract of territory so that it was impossible for the Superintendent of Bakers to direct and oversee all matters from the van to the rear, over the entire line of march. Also, he sagely remarked, "It is often impossible for one man, who is otherwise sufficiently occupied," to find masons, lime, and bricks and direct the proper building of ovens. The question of the expense of this oven building was also to be settled. Congress met Ludwick's recommendation by placing a fund of one thousand dollars in his hands, with which to build ovens as he saw fit and authorized him to employ any workmen he thought proper to do the work. It gave him authority to demand flour from any commissary or military storekeeper, directed him to pay the bakers he employed and to draw on the Paymaster-General for settlement of his accounts, and designated the Commissary-General of Issues, or his deputy, as the officer to receive the bread; lastly it directed the Quartermaster-General of the Army to furnish the Commissary-General of Issues with a sufficient number of covered wagons, of one-ton capacity, that could be locked, or fastened up, in which the bread was to be transported. There are few instances of such complete acquiescence on the part of the Continental Congress in the recommendations of an officer, other than that attention it paid to the recommendations of the Commander-in-Chief.

The need for bread at the opening of the campaign of 1777 was pressing, and Washington sent Ludwick to Philadelphia to lay the situation before Congress. As a result of his representations, it was ordered that supplies of flour, previously directed to be sold, be baked into "bisket" as fast as possible and that the bakers in Philadelphia be urged to help. The Commissary-General of Purchases was directed to have all the flour in his stores at Lancaster, Downingtown, and Valley Forge converted into bread. Ludwick could not obtain bakers enough for this activity because most of the journeymen bakers in Philadelphia were serving in the Pennsylvania militia, so Congress recommended to the Supreme Executive Council of that State, that as many bakers in the militia as Ludwick called for be excused from military service for the time he needed them.

The main group of Ludwick's ovens seems to have been built at Morristown, New Jersey, where he had started building them before the army moved from that place. Other small groups were scattered along the route of march in Jersey and at convenient places in Pennsylvania. The establishment of these various baking-posts was decided by the movements of the army and the convenience of the roads. And, though all of them worked steadily with the resources at their command, the bread supply of the army was seldom more than a few days, or a week, ahead of the consumption.

After obtaining Congressional action, Ludwick left Philadelphia and hastened to Pottstown, there to be met by a letter from the Commander-in-Chief, ordering him to send every bit of bread he had to Coryell's Ferry, except two thousand pounds which was to be sent to White Horse Tavern to await the arrival of the troops that were with Washington himself. Two divisions were to pass through Pottstown and would want bread. The Commander-in-Chief gave Ludwick authority to hire or impress wagons to bring the bread to the troops and asked where the new ovens would be erected so no time would be lost in sending for bread as it was needed. At the same time that he gave these orders to Ludwick, Washington directed the Quartermaster-General to put all the private bakers in Philadelphia to work baking hard bread. A week later the Commander-in-Chief sent a hurry call to Ludwick to come to camp at once; to leave an experienced baker in charge of the Morristown ovens, and, to sweep up, on his way, all the bread he found at Coryell's and Pottstown and send it forward to the army. The need was great; as the Quartermaster-General had not been successful in getting the private bakers in Philadelphia to work for the army, Washington requested that Ludwick try to accomplish the same thing.

The transportation difficulty had been anticipated and measures were taken by Washington to meet it, in some degree, by orders to construct portable ovens of sheet iron, light enough in weight to be easily carried. These ovens were made at the Ringwood iron furnace and were so small that two of them could be carried on an army wagon. The idea was good, the purpose was laudable, but the ovens, ordered in June, did not reach the army until near the end of November, 1777. By then, what with the fighting and continuous maneuvering to save Philadelphia, the lines of supply had broken, all the reserve stocks exhausted and Major-General Greene complained that the army was living from hand to mouth, at the very beginning of what was to prove that most terrible winter at Valley Forge. Before the army had fairly settled into winter quarters the pinch was felt, and a brigadier-general who was directed to hold his brigade in readiness to march, wrote that he welcomed the orders, as fighting would be preferable to starving. The failure of provisions was most severely felt in the flour supply and another brigadier wrote to the Commander-in-Chief that for three successive days his troops had been without bread, and he doubted if the men could be held much longer. "According to the saying of Solomon," he wrote, "hunger will break through a stone wall," and, indeed, it was a marvel that the Continental Army was held together during the winter of 1777–78.

It was the experiences of this terrible winter that finally showed Congress the need of providing a permanent staff of bakers. Ludwick was doing his best, but greater official sanction seemed necessary. In February, 1778, Congress ordered the enlistment of a company of bakers, to be managed by a director, who would be paid fifty dollars a month and three rations per day, three sub-directors at forty dollars and two rations, twelve foremen at thirty dollars and one ration, and sixty-four bakers at twenty-four dollars and one ration. The term of enlistment was to be one year and the articles of war were to govern. A clothing allowance the same as that of the non-commissioned officers was granted and the Board of War was directed to appoint the director and sub-directors and raise the company as speedily as possible. This organization was in addition to Ludwick's arrangements and was not supposed to interfere with him in any way.

The attempted remedy failed. The Board of War dodged the responsibility by placing the matter in the hands of Major-General William Heath, then commanding the Eastern Department. He raised the company in Boston and appointed John Torrey to be its captain. This company was sent to camp in June, 1778. Soon after Torrey arrived, the army broke camp with speed and started its forced march across Jersey in pursuit of the British. The rapidity of the succeeding events seemed to have dazed Torrey somewhat. He gave it as his positive opinion that camp was an improper place for baking hard bread. He had expected to bake soft bread, but nobody wanted it except the staff officers. Every brigade had found means to bake for itself (that the means were Ludwick's arrangements did not seem to be understood) also, because the men made a little saving, or profit, by drawing flour for their rations instead of soft bread, soft bread was never called for even when hard bread could not be obtained. The idea was to save this profit by means of Torrey's company, but Torrey's idea of the necessary preparations at every camping-place of a moving army cost as much as would be necessary for a whole year's business. The captain of the bakers was a well-meaning and honest patriot, but he did not seem to be equal to military emergencies. He suggested that he be allowed to return to Boston and bake biscuit, or hard bread there. When the matter was referred to Washington, he settled it by ordering Torrey's men to establish a permanent baking-station at Springfield, Massachusetts, where the largest manufacturing post and supply arsenal of the Revolutionary War was located. The United States Government still retains an important supply post there. By August, 1778, the expense of this baking-station had amounted to six thousand dollars.

All the difficulties of the bread supply, as managed by Ludwick, centered around the question of flour.

Periods of prolonged drought which withered crops and dried up the water-power in the mills; long continued and heavy rains which hurt the grain, clogged the roads, and held up the supply wagons; speculators who gambled in foodstuffs, and farmers who held on to their grain for better prices, all contributed to the hardships suffered by the army.

There was always sufficient food in America to feed the Continental troops bountifully; transportation and mismanagement, most of which were avoidable, kept the army nearly always in want. The quantity of the bread ration was cut down many times to eke out the supply during periods of scarcity. Several times during the year 1779, and not always during the winter months, the Northern Department troops were on the verge of mutiny from lack of bread. The ragged finances of the central Government were responsible, in large measure, for the bread scarcity. Purchasing agents strained their personal credit to the breaking-point to obtain flour. Some idea of the consumption of this article may be had from the statement of the Commissary-General that seven hundred barrels of flour would furnish the army with bread for only two weeks. By July, 1780, Ludwick had demonstrated that no flour should be issued at all, as a part of the daily ration; nothing but hard bread should be issued. Ovens were erected at West Point and Stony Point, in addition to those at Fishkill; the New Jersey and Pennsylvania posts, and those at West Point became the final baking-stations of the Continental Army. They had a capacity of eight thousand pounds of hard bread a day.

The beginning of the year 1781 brought something of a crisis in bread-baking. Ludwick had been struggling desperately to maintain the bread supply, but the breakdown of the specific supply system and the confusion in inaugurating the new contract scheme for feeding the army were too much for the old man. He had suffered a crippling accident, and, despite his saving even the sweepings of the flour barrels and gaining a little by selling the empty barrels themselves, he was unable to obtain flour. By his economies and carefulness he had kept the yearly expense of bread-baking below three thousand pounds and "Advanced in years [he was sixty-one in 1781], blind in one eye and almost worn out in the service of his country," was the pitiful way in which he introduced himself to Congress and begged leave to resign. All of his bakers had left him, except those few civilians he was retaining by advancing their pay out of his own pocket; the two master bakers, one of them Torrey, who had been appointed by order of Congress, had given up and left the whole burden on Ludwick's shoulders. He reminded Congress that he had

served His Country honestly from the Commencement of the War [the first six months as a volunteer, finding himself and Horse without fee or reward] — built the greatest part of the Bakehouses for the use of the Army; —

ventur'd his Life on several occasions for the Cause; — had
his property ruined by the Enemy; — expended his private fortune, earned by his industry before the War; and
by his Assiduity and Vigilance in his Department saved
great sums of money to the States; and he is now willing
and desirous to retire from the Service in the sixty-first
year of his Age, with the loss of his right eye and a ruined
Constitution.

But Congress declined to accept his resignation.
He was authorized to call for money from the military
chest of the Commander-in-Chief, and it was voted
that

he had acted with great industry and integrity in the character of principal Superintendent of Bakers . . . that he be
empowered to hire any number of bakers, not exceeding
thirty, and that he receive as compensation for all past
services, one thousand dollars in bills of the new emission.

A board of general officers considered the baking
situation in June, 1781, and advised the use of traveling ovens for each brigade, and that one and one
quarter pounds of bread should be required of every
pound of flour. It is indicative of the general lack of
system that this board of 1781 should recommend the
use of traveling ovens that had been ordered and
experimented with in 1778. The opening of the
campaign of 1781, brought forth orders from the
Commander-in-Chief, to start up all the ovens and all
the available bakers to baking hard bread as speedily
as possible. With a good reserve in hand, the combined American and French armies commenced their

march southward. It was by means of the French bakers that Washington was able to mislead Sir Henry Clinton so that the British general believed New York City was to be attacked and, not until the allies had reached Philadelphia did he awake to the knowledge that their object was Cornwallis, in Virginia. Then it was too late to check Washington.

The French bakers, under orders, set up ovens and made great preparation and bustle at Chatham, New Jersey, and a guard of Continentals was placed around the establishment and held there until September 2d, by which date Washington had reached Philadelphia and the ruse was completely successful. After the surrender of Cornwallis and the return of the Continental Army to the Hudson River, the contract system of feeding the army began to produce results; Ludwick nevertheless continued his baking operations at West Point. Almost immediately the contractors proposed modifications in the terms of the contract, and almost the first modifications had to do with the bread supply. It was proposed to increase the bread ration by half a pound and furnish two pounds of soap for every one hundred rations in return for withholding one half of the daily ration of rum; but this was not because of temperance principles. This proposal started trouble, for, from the very beginning, the quality of the bread issued by the contractors had been poor. Ludwick had kept steadily at work at West Point, and when, at the close of the year 1782, the contract scheme was abandoned, the bread supply of the army was safe. The troops were gradually disbanded during the summer of 1783 and, as the army dwindled in size, the bread supply became an ever easier matter to handle. Long before New York City was finally evacuated by the British, the arrangements and methods of Ludwick were amply sufficient for all the strain put upon them.

The importance of Ludwick's work to the efficiency of the Continental Army was such that he deserves to be held in much better remembrance than is the case at present. The value of his services is certified to by Major-Generals Anthony Wayne, Thomas Mifflin, and Arthur St. Clair and Colonels William Irvine and Timothy Pickering. Last of all General Washington himself certified that he had

known Christopher Ludwick from an early period in the war, and have every reason to believe, as well from observation as information, that he has been a true and faithful servant to the public; that he has detected and exposed many impositions, which were attempted to be practiced by others in his department; that he has been the cause of much saving in many respects; and that his deportment in public life has afforded unquestionable proofs of his integrity and worth.

And when George Washington wrote thus about a fellow patriot no further praise is needed.

Ludwick died a year and a half after Washington, and a final touch is given in the answer he gave to a book canvasser who tried to sell him a life of his old

Commander-in-Chief, shortly after Washington's death. It illustrates in clear colors the comradeship and human understanding that existed between Washington and those men of the Revolution whom he had tried and found not wanting. Ludwick's answer to the request that he subscribe for a copy of the life was: "No, I will not, I am traveling fast to meet him, and I will soon hear all about it from his own lips."

From the quaint old tombstone in the Lutheran Church at Germantown, where Ludwick lies, comes this message:

On every occasion his zeal for the relief of the oppressed was manifest; and by his last will, he bequeathed the greater part of his estate for the education of the children of the poor of all denominations, gratis. He lived and died respected for his integrity and public spirit, by all who knew him. Reader, such was Ludwick. Art thou poor, Venerate his character. Art thou rich, Imitate his example.

X

THE BANDS OF THE CONTINENTAL ARMY

THE elaborate military brass band of to-day has little in common with "The Spirit of '76," for the military music of the Revolutionary War was nothing more than what we should call a drum and fife corps and rather a small one at that. But it was a most valuable adjunct to the fighting rank and file, and it is questionable if a smile of fancied superiority is justified at the thought of it. Of course we have heard fife and drum corps; at times, if fortunate, we have heard what are called good ones; but we cannot be sure that we have ever heard one that is really as good as the drums and fifes that swung through the streets of old Philadelphia when Washington was marching to cut off Cornwallis at Yorktown; that squealed down the Jersey road when he pounded after Clinton's retreating troops; or that filled in the hoarse cheer of the charge at Monmouth, swirling it to a shrill scream of triumph, punctuated by the crash of musket and cannon-shot.

The drums and fifes of the Continental Army were taken very seriously by the men of the Revolution, and their contribution to the service, the discipline and efficiency of the army was very real. The appeal of uniforms, arms and flags would not carry so easily without the drums and fifes to wake them into life and action. The scraping thud of marching feet, the flutter and snap of the colors gain vividness and spirit from the rhythmic tap of the drum and the high, clear shrill of the fife.

The camp and garrison calls of our army have long been given by the bugle, an instrument almost unknown in America during the Revolution, though the dragoons, or cavalry, had a trumpet. The late World War developed a system of whistle and silent arm signals for the march and battlefield that supplanted other sound orders for obvious reasons; but the Continental Army took its orders from the drum. By the drum it rose in the morning, assembled, paraded, saluted, marched off, ceased work, and retired for the night. These signals (termed "calls" for the bugle) were known as "beats" for the drum. The principal ones were the Reveille, the General, the Assembly, the Retreat (at sunset, which was the finish of the day's work, when all troops returned to their barracks, or encampment), and the older Taptoo, later Tattoo and now Taps, which originally meant to put the tap to or close the tap or drinking vats of the public tavern, which, necessarily was the signal for closing the tavern. Taps, then, as a military meaning, is "lights out" for the night. These were the principal "beats"; there were others, of course, which will be mentioned later, but these were the main signals of the military day.

The drum itself, with which these signals were given, was much like our present-day instrument (bearing in mind that the huge bass drum was unknown to the Continental Army), but differing from it in size, proportion, and weight. It was a snare drum, so called from the gut strings, or snares, stretched across the bottom, which add to the resonance and give a timbre to the vibrations impossible to obtain in any other way. The diameter of the Revolutionary drum was only slightly larger than that of to-day, but it was about three times as long and its side was of wood; the usual cords, laced into the head and base rims were held tight by sliding leather clips and kept the skin drumheads taut. The drum was carried, as now, in front of the body, against the left leg, supported by a shoulder belt and slings in such manner as to incline its head at a proper angle for easy beating.

The fifer was inseparable from the drummer when the army was on the march, and his fife differed little from the fife of to-day; it was a little larger, a little cruder in workmanship and finish, but that was all. The uniform of both drummer and fifer was the same as that of the regiment to which they belonged, and they carried no arms of any kind. Together the drums and fifes, twenty to thirty each to a regiment, constituted the bands, or "music" of the army. The terms "music" and "musician" in the Continental Army are somewhat confusing to us because of the great advances made in the invention and manufacture of band instruments since the days of Seventy-Six. Then the distinction apparently was one of numbers. If there were only three or four drums and fifes grouped together they were merely "drums and fifes" or the "music"; if there were from ten to fifteen or more of each, it was then a "band." Colonel Christian Febiger, of the Second Virginia Regiment, in a letter to the Commander-in-Chief, in February, 1782, wrote that his bandsmen were enlisted as "musicians and fifers," a curious distinction, and though some of the army returns distinguish drummers, fifers, and musicians, no returns of supplies mention any musical instruments other than drums and fifes.

In the British army many of the bands by 1776 and later had evolved beyond the drum and fife, and by 1783 the British Guard regiments generally boasted of bands consisting of oboes, clarinets, horns, and bassoons in addition to drums and fifes. But these wind instruments were unknown to the Continentals, who possessed no musicians skillful enough to play them. A delightful commentary upon this situation and the then new instruments is found in Major-General Henry Knox's report on the British stores captured at Stony Point. To Knox was assigned the appraisement of the captured property in order that the Light Infantry might be paid the prize money awarded them for their brilliant exploit and, while the chief of artillery was perfectly conversant with the value of cannon, shell, powder, rammers, carcasses, caissons, and such, he was completely at sea when he encountered two French horns, two bassoons, and two clarinets. He wrote down that he was unacquainted with the value of these, but, as he had heard that the Light Infantry was offered one thousand dollars for them, he, therefore, naïvely appraised them at one thousand dollars.

So far as America was concerned the progress of military music was slow. The author of an old work on this class of harmony, published some years after the Revolutionary War says in his preface:

Martial music has been too generally considered, not only by people in general, but by military characters as an object of small importance and worthy of but little of their attention and encouragement . . . and . . . notwithstanding its . . . utility . . . it has remained with us in a very low and depressed state.

However, there was proper appreciation of the value of the drum and fife music by the Commander-in-Chief, and, indeed, there is a deal of evidence to show that Washington not only recognized the military value and utility of music, but that he took personal pleasure in hearing it, and that this liking extended to all kinds of music with which he was acquainted. It was a common knowledge in the army of this partiality of the Commander-in-Chief for melody that brought about the first public recognition of Washington's birthday. This occurred at Valley Forge when the bandsmen of Procter's Artillery marched over the frozen road of that gloomy encampment, down into the bleak valley, bravely paraded before Headquarters in the biting cold and chill, and serenaded their Commander-in-Chief. It was a military compliment that Washington would not let pass unnoticed, and from the scanty funds in his possession he ordered a small gratuity of "hard money" distributed to the doughty players in recognition of their efforts. It may be of passing interest to know the names of the men who were the first publicly to celebrate Washington's birthday. They appear on the returns of Colonel Procter's regiment as follows: Drum Major William Norton; Fife Major Thomas Guy; Music Master Charles Hoffman; Musicians William Shippen, Peter Colkhoffer, Jacob Snell, Thomas Mingle, George Weaver; Drummers John Spade, Henry Gregor, Hugh Fegan, George Thompson, Thomas Connelly, Michael King, William McDaniel; Fifers Jacob Smith, James Crutcher, David Broderick, Michael Clingan, Jacob Bryan, and Robert Patterson. All of these were Pennsylvanians except Fifer Patterson, who was from New Jersey and enlisted in Trenton; Hoffman, Colkhoffer, and Weaver, though Pennsylvanians, had been born in Germany; Clingan had been born in London and Drum Major Norton in Ireland.

It was the fifes, of course, that furnished the music, so-called; the drums added the color and emphasis. It does not appear that the drummers ever had any sheet music or practiced from written notes. The army returns of the Revolution show that the fifers were furnished with music sheets on which the music was written or copied out by the fife majors, who kept record of the established marches and other pieces in blank books which were furnished them for preserving the original scores against loss by accident. It is regrettable that none of these score books seem to have survived.

But while the fifes were the real music of the Continental Army, the drums were the more important instruments. The method of playing, the various strokes used by the Revolutionary drummer have not been greatly added to or developed by later knowledge. The principal strokes or taps were the "flam," the "roll," and the "drag." The "flam" was a light tap followed by a hard one with the other stick; the "roll" was two clean, sharp strokes with one stick followed by two similar strokes with the other, alternating as rapidly as need be; the "drag" was one hard stroke with one stick, then two light strokes with the other, and alternating the hard strokes with either hand. The possible combinations of these strokes are almost infinite, and an early American treatise warns that "the drummer should be careful never to fill up the beat or march with unnecessary or superfluous strokes or rolls, as any more than are necessary to keep the time correctly and coincide with the air of the tune for which the beat is intended is highly disgusting."

Among the pieces necessary for the drummer to learn was a slow march, a parade march, a funeral march, the quick step, the "troop," sometimes used as the assembly, which was specially a British march, to the time of a slow waltz and was nicknamed by the soldiers the "Ladies Parade"; the cadence of this was about seventy-two to the minute. The quick step, or ordinary marching pace was about one hundred and twenty to the minute; the double time or old double quick was about one hundred and forty to the minute. As to the titles of the various popular airs played by the Continental Army "bands," it is not possible to give them with any degree of certainty. "Yankee Doodle" was, of course, quite well known and doubtless often played after 1777; but there is no evidence to show that it was a prime favorite with the military. Of the titles of pieces that have survived since the War of 1812, we cannot be sure that many of them were popular or even known in the days of the Revolution.

The drum major was in charge of the entire band (both drums and fifes) while on parade or march; he selected the pieces to be played and governed the starting and stopping of the music. He carried a cane or staff that was not so very different from that now used. There was a fife major whose office does not now exist in the army. He had charge of the fifes, saw to their proficiency, and ordered all things connected with them. He necessarily had to be more of a musician than the drum major, but was under the latter's command at all times when the drums and fifes were together. The drums are first noticed in the general orders of the Commander-in-Chief, July 14, 1775, eleven days after he took command of the army, in fixing the honors to be paid to the general officers by the guards. The Commander-in-Chief was to be received with rested arms and the drums were to beat a march; a major general was received with rested arms and the drums beat two ruffles; a brigadier-general received the same arms honor and the drums beat one ruffle. The "ruffle" was a short roll, played in a subdued tone. This regulation was modified in May, 1778, so far as it applied to the Commander-in-Chief, by omitting the drum honor whenever the troops were near the enemy, as it was considered unwise thus to announce the presence of the head of the army to the British.

The pay of drummers and fifers was fixed by Congress July 29, 1775, as the same as that of a corporal, seven and one-third dollars per month. The war was a year old before the matter of the pay of the drum and fife majors was settled, although their exact regimental status seemed to have been a matter of some doubt for the entire period of the war. Washington objected to following the practice of the British army, which was to increase the pay of the drum and fife majors above that of the drummers and fifers by stoppages of small amounts from the pay of the rank and file. It would, he thought, cause uneasiness and trouble, and he suggested to the Board of War that the pay of these music directors be increased to one dollar a month more than that of the common soldier. This was done, and, later, this small increase was cannily sequestered under the specious plea of economy.

The Continental Army drummer seemed to be a persistent enthusiast in his determination to master the art of making rhythmic noise. He reveled in every opportunity to drum vehemently, and, in October, 1776, a general order was directed against him. He was forbidden to beat his drum except on parade and main guard, the practice of marching the fatigue parties to their work with a full compliment of drums and fifes playing gayly, was stopped and after retreat no drums were allowed to beat on any account. The drummer practiced at any time he felt the spirit move him, and the harassed soldier did not know whether he should fly to arms or not. A regular practice hour for drumming was set later on and, at Valley Forge, as spring advanced, this hour was put forward and the drummers allowed to drum from 5 to 6 A.M., and from 4 to 5 P.M. Practicing at any other times than these incurred severe penalty, the matter being put before the troops by general orders in this wise:

The use of drums are as signals to the army, and if every drummer is allowed to beat at his pleasure the intention is entirely destroyed, as it will be impossible to distinguish whether they are beating for their own pleasure or for a signal to the troops.

That our forefathers sometimes developed cases of "nerves" over the frequent hullabaloo of the drum enthusiasts is evident from Major-General Heath's orders in Boston during the month of May, 1777. The inhabitants complained of Sabbath-Day practicing, and Heath ordered that the beating of drums on the Lord's Day (except for certain special reasons) be omitted. A few days later the honorable the General Court complained that the frequent beating of drums around the court-house interrupted the debates, and, it appearing that the eloquence of the legislators was a much more important noise than that caused by a well-beaten drum, all drumming was forbidden while the legislature was sitting "(except on special occasions), either for practice or on duty."

A good picture of the place of the drum in the daily life of the camp is found in the orders of Captain Leonard Bleeker to the troops encamped at Canajoharie Creek, June 18, 1779. Captain Bleeker evidently had had some trouble with his drummers and drumming, and he straightened matters out in the following manner:

For the future, until further orders, one drummer will be for duty from each regiment, and the daily beats shall be as follows: The different daily beats shall begin on the right of the camp, and be instantly followed by the whole army, to facilitate which, the drummer's call shall be beat by the drummer then on duty of each regiment a quarter of an hour before the time of beating, when the drummers will assemble before the colors of their respective regiments, and as soon as the beat begins on the right, it shall be instantly taken up by the whole army. The drummers beating along the front of their respective regiments, from the center to the right, from thence to the left, and back again to the center, where they finish. The different beats and signals are to be as follows. The General is to beat only when the whole is to march, and is the signal to strike the tents and prepare for the march. The Assembly is the signal to repair to the colors, the March, for the whole to move. The Reveille is to beat at daybreak, and is the signal for the soldiers to rise, and the sentries to leave off challenging. The Troop assembles the soldiers together for the purpose of calling the roll and inspecting the men for duty, it will begin tomorrow at half after seven in the morning, and the men ordered for duty, to be on the grand parade at eight o'clock. The Retreat is to beat at sunset for calling the roll, warning the men for duty, and reading the orders of the day. The Tattoo is for the soldiers to repair to their tents, where they must remain until Reveille beating the next morning, unless ordered otherwise. To Arms, is a signal for getting under arms in case of an alarm. The Parley is to desire a conference with the enemy.

The marching regulations laid down by General Washington for the main army, ordered that the "drummers are to beat the first division of the foot march to be taken from the front to the rear and upon the last *flam* of the first division being struck, the whole are to march." The drummers on the march were forbidden to put their drums into the wagons, just as the rank and file, unless they were sick or lame, were forbidden so to stow their muskets. If detected in such an attempt, they were to be flogged on the spot.

There was a scarcity of drums and fifes throughout the war, and many were the complaints and calls for a supply of the first-mentioned instrument. The thin wooden sides of the drums made them particularly vulnerable, and a large number of them were broken and out of repair at all times. The Continental Board of War finally found means to have drums made, but even after this was arranged a scarcity of materials continued to cause delays. The Commissary of Artillery reported to Washington, in January, 1777, in despairing tones that he had no drums to issue except forty broken ones; that not two of these were fit for service, and that he had no heads or other materials with which to repair them.

In August, 1778, the music of the army was put upon a consistent basis by the appointment of an Inspector, or Superintendent of Music, for the entire army. Lieutenant John Hiwill, of Crane's Artillery Regiment, was appointed to this position by general orders of the Commander-in-Chief, August 19th, and held the position until the disbanding of the Continental Army. While he still retained his lieutenant's rank, he was given the pay and rations of a captain of artillery. This was one of the unique appointments of the war and was the beginning of the systematizing of the music of the army. There were many difficulties to be smoothed over and the new Inspector's days were full of activity. The main trouble lay in the lack of drums and fifes and a secondary difficulty was the lack of uniformity in the status of the musicians. An example of this was the trouble over Colonel Henry Jackson's regimental band. Washington wrote to Major-General John Sullivan, December 20, 1778, that a band was no part of the army establishment and no privileges could be granted Jackson's musicians without causing difficulties with other regiments.

It seems odd that a band was no part of the army establishment, when an Inspector of Music had been appointed four months prior to this statement from Washington, but such was the fact. Drummers and fifers were practical necessities in the army and means had been found to obtain them and continue them from the beginning of the war; but their status was somewhat akin to independent or partisan troops, though they lacked the coherent organized entity even of these. They were strictly non-combatants who did not appear to possess any of the specified qualifications of the common soldier. It is but another example of the general looseness of the Revolutionary organization. Difficulty arose on this score in the third year of the war by the drummers and fifers refusing to do guard, sentry, police, and other duties of the soldier, and the Board of War recommended to Congress that all able-bodied drummers and fifers be obliged to do duty as soldiers and that they be furnished with arms. Unfortunately for this hasty recommendation of method, the enlistment agreements, under which the drummers and fifers were secured, blocked such summary exercise of slapdash authority, and the matter was not settled until many months later.

After the Board of War was replaced by the appointment of a Secretary of War, this tangle of enlistment agreement and soldier duty again arose, and the Secretary of War wrote to Congress, December 21, 1781, that the method heretofore used for enlisting men as drummers and fifers with additional pay injured the service. Men fit for the ranks escaped the duties of soldiers by engaging as drummers and fifers, while boys, hardly able to bear arms, were drafted into the ranks. He recommended to Congress that no men be enlisted as drummers and fifers, but that commanding officers be given authority to draft men from the ranks for that purpose with such additional pay as the commanding officers saw fit to order them. But the Secretary thriftily suggested that this additional pay be stopped from the soldier and used as a fund to keep the drums and fifes in repair. This suggestion appealed to Congressional economy, so it was ordered that in future no recruit should be enlisted to serve as a drummer or fifer. When such were needed, they were to be taken from the ranks in such numbers and of such description as the Commander-in-Chief, or the commanding officer of a separate army, should direct and be returned back to the ranks and others drawn out as often as the good of the service made necessary. A good drum and fife were to be furnished to each musician, but that stoppages out of his pay should be made to keep the instruments in good order.

When the French Army arrived at Rhode Island, the Continental drums and fifes were thrown somewhat in the background by the more showy bands of Rochambeau's force. On Washington's visit to Newport in March, 1781, to confer with the French commander, the French officers arranged a ball in his honor. They decorated the ballroom with flags, swords, drums, streamers, and all the fanciful color that the army possessed, and General Washington opened the ball by request. He danced the first number with Miss Margaret Champlin, one of the reigning belles of Newport, and, as the signal was given, the French officers took the instruments from the hands of their musicians and flourished the opening strains of "A Successful Campaign," which piece Miss Champlin had chosen as the one with which the ball should open. The fife music of this old and popular Revolutionary composition has survived and is here given:

It proved a prophetic choice, for eight months afterwards the two generals present at that Newport ball finished a successful campaign by forcing the surrender of Cornwallis at Yorktown; a defeat so crushing in its effects and so humiliating to the troops involved that the British bands, permitted to play a British march while the ranks moved out to surrender, attempted a satire by viciously beating out upon their drums "The World Turned Upside Down." But instead of satire those drums were, all unconsciously, beating a powerful truth into the ears of the entire world, for they were announcing the beginning of the end of monarchy as a system of government and, in the year 1781, that truly was a world turned upside down.

After Yorktown the Continental Army began to take real definite shape as a disciplined, fighting machine. The experiences of seven years of war were beginning to tell, and nowhere do the results show more clearly than in the general orders of the Commander-in-Chief. A tightening of discipline is plainly evident, and the loose ends of the army were caught up and woven into the military fabric as never had been the case before. Contact with the trained veterans of France probably helped largely by furnishing a standard, but, whatever the cause, a more systematic routine of management is evident. The Inspector of Music was ordered to perform his duties in conjunction with the Inspector-General of the Army, to be present with the Inspectors and report to the Commander-in-Chief the condition and number of the instruments. This report disclosed such a deficiency of drums and fifes that Inspector Hiwill was sent on a special mission to the Secretary of War in Philadelphia to lay the matter personally before that official. He was ordered to stay in Philadelphia, if necessary, and lend his aid and advice in the manufacture of the instruments. In August, 1782, he was ordered to see to it that there was exact uniformity in the different "beats" throughout the entire army. Drum signals were to be continually made use of and pointedly attended to. The drum and fife majors were to assemble daily and receive instruction from the Inspector of Music, and this was to continue until they were perfect in their duties. By this it seems evident that, even as late as 1782, there was a noticeable lack of skill among the bandmasters, and in one of Hiwill's reports there is to be found this delicious bit: "N.B. The Fife Majors and Fifers of the 5th Regt. are in bad order."

The value of the band in the army, as well as the difficulties under which it often struggled, are well portrayed in a letter from Colonel Febiger, March 14, 1782, to Washington. He had tried to raise a band, but had had such small success that he conceived the notion of inducing British and German deserters to serve as such. He soon found that no dependence could be placed upon these, so he next tried to train native youths; boys too young for military service in the ranks. He succeeded in forming a band of eight, though he could not obtain these recruits without promising the soldier's bounty, clothing and rations. He paid for the drums and fifes out of his own pocket, and then the Board of War refused to reimburse him for the outlay on the ground that every regiment would make similar claims even though it did not take any pains to raise a band. Febiger proudly stated that his youths' "music had more influence on the minds and motions of the militia last summer in this state than would the oratory of a Cicero, & in the recruiting business they are at least as useful as a well spoken recruiting sergeant."

After Yorktown the Continental Army marched north, leaving the French to winter in Virginia, and the next summer the French moved north and joined the Continentals on the banks of the Hudson. The American troops were at Newburgh and they moved down the river, to join the French at Verplanck's Point, in boats. Practically the entire army went down by water, and only the artillery and heavy baggage marched by land to King's Ferry. This was the first grand water maneuver of the army, and it was accomplished without delay or hitch in one day. The troops moved down to the boats and embarked according to plan in which the drums and fifes played an important part. After all were embarked and the lines formed, the rear brigade beat a march which was taken up and repeated to the head of the line. Three cannon shot were then fired from the artillery park at West Point and the boats immediately got into motion. The carrying power of the Continental drum and fife is well attested by this, for it is evident that

the music carried from the vicinity of Newburgh
through the Highlands to the ears of the waiting
artillerymen at West Point. Blue and white flags
were flown at front and rear of the column of boats to
regulate the speed, and the bands of the different regiments were ordered to play alternately throughout
the line. Inspector Hiwill had charge of this and
regulated the "beats."

Never has the Hudson River beheld so beautiful a
picture as when the army that gained liberty for a
nation came down its broad bosom that August morning. The early morning sun sparkled upon the river
and bathed in splendor the massive cliffs of Storm
King and Crow's Nest. At the foot of these mighty
buttresses of the Hudson Highlands, where the river
narrows to a cool, shadowed curve, the mile-long line
of buff-and-blue-filled craft wound through that age-
old waterway; bayonets sun-tipped with silver, flags
fluttering and snapping in the breeze and the stirring
music of drums and fifes dancing cheerily across the
sparkling water to echo sweetly back from the green
and purple heights far above.

The movement was so perfectly carried out that
Washington thanked the army in general orders the
following day. Shortly thereafter a grand review was
held in honor of Comte Rochambeau. He was met at
King's Ferry by a dragoon guard of honor and escorted through the entire American Army, drawn up
in two lines, facing each other fully clothed and

equipped, for the first time during the war, with supplies furnished by France. During the entire maneuvers of the day all the marches played by the Continental bands were French.

Practically the last regulation issued for the music was given in general orders at Verplanck's Point in September, 1782, fixing the position of the drum and fife when the guards marched by platoons. The music was to dress on the front rank of the first platoon, the drum to the right of the sergeant and the fife to the right of the drum. When the Continental Army finally disbanded, the men of the rank and file were allowed to retain their muskets; the drummers and fifers thought they should also be given arms and, as they had been drafted from the ranks, the Secretary of War thought this idea reasonable. Congress thought otherwise and forbade arms being given to the musicians. They were allowed to take home with them their drums and fifes, and that was all.

Little of the military music of the Revolution has survived; but in the back of an old book of fife music the writer was fortunate enough to discover a few pages of manuscript and one of them bore the title "Old Continental March." It is here given:

XI

THE INVALID REGIMENT AND ITS COLONEL

AN organization unique in American military history was the regiment of invalids commanded by Colonel Lewis Nicola, of Pennsylvania. This experiment in providing for the wounded and disabled of the Revolutionary armies has interest for us to-day as the first crude attempt in what has now developed into a scientifically directed salvaging of war-wrecked humanity.

Colonel Nicola, the commanding officer of the corps, was a unique character. Born in Dublin, of Huguenot ancestry, he entered the British Army when twenty-three years old, rose to the rank of major, came to America eighteen years before the Revolution, and settled in Philadelphia. A man of no mean talents, a surveyor and engineer, he was a member of the American Philosophical Society and at one time the editor of its publications. When the Revolutionary War broke out, he was fifty-eight years old, and, being strongly in favor of the cause of the Colonies, he was made Barrackmaster-General of Philadelphia in 1776 and acted as town-major from that year to 1782. At the close of his Revolutionary services he held the brevet-rank of brigadier-general. When the war commenced, he immediately translated an important French work on military engineering

and had it printed in Philadelphia along with a
treatise of his own on "Military Exercise Calculated
for the Use of the Americans." But he is best remembered as the man who proposed to Washington
that he proclaim himself king and use the army to set
up a monarchy as the form of government best calculated to meet the situation that had developed in
the year 1782.

Fourteen months of war had passed before Congress took up the matter of permanent provision for
wounded and disabled men. A committee consisting
of Robert Treat Paine, Francis Lightfoot Lee, Hyman
Hall, William Ellery, and Francis Lewis was appointed to consider what provision ought to be made
for disabled soldiers and seamen, and their report resulted in the resolution of August 26, 1776, to grant
half-pay for life or during the continuance of the dis-
ability, a chief misfortune seeming to be that of the
loss of a limb. By this resolve also the Invalid Corps
was created. It was to be composed of all disabled
officers and soldiers who were found to be capable of
doing guard or garrison duty; the seamen to be simi-
larly incorporated and employed.

There appears to be no record of the result of this
experiment so far as the navy is concerned, but the
army regiment was duly formed in 1777 as a corps of
eight companies of one hundred men each, not including the commissioned and non-commissioned officers.
Their specific duties were to act as garrisons and

guards in cities and places where magazines of supplies were located. The regiment was to serve also as
a military school for young gentlemen previous to
their being appointed to the marching regiments, and
all the subaltern officers while off duty were obliged to
attend a mathematical school to learn "Geometry,
Arithmetick, vulgar and decimal Fractions and the
extraction of Roots." The officers of the corps were
obliged to contribute one day's pay each month for
the purchase of a regimental library "of the most approved Authors on Tacticks and the Petite Guere."
So, in a sense, the Invalid Regiment was the first military school of the United States Army, a faint and
shadowy precursor of West Point, while the method
devised for creating the first official military library in
the United States showed a canny sense of thrift on
the part of our colonial Congressmen, whatever else
may be thought of it.

Some officers of the Invalid Corps were to be constantly employed in the recruiting service and all
recruits obtained were to be brought into the corps,
trained, drilled, and then drafted into the field regiments. A month after the corps was established, June
20, 1777, Congress directed the surgeons of the hospitals to see to it that before men were discharged from
the hospitals as unfit for further service, it be considered whether or not such men might be capable of
garrison duty, and if so found to transfer them to the
Invalid Corps. The Board of War was directed to

send notice of the creation of the corps to all commanding generals that such men as were still with the regiments, but were unfit for active duty, might be properly transferred. Men having only one arm or one leg each were deemed proper recruits. An advertisement was ordered published calling on all men in the service who were incapable of field duties either by reason of wounds or disorders to present themselves to Colonel Nicola in Front Street, Philadelphia. If they were judged fit for the corps, they were immediately put upon full pay. Officers who desired transfer to the corps were obliged to furnish certificates of their physical condition, and no officer would be received who could not produce ample testimony of having served with reputation and possessing a good character both as a soldier and a citizen. Officers and men who had enlisted for the war were given the preference.

The corps was formed and with Colonel Nicola as its directing spirit struggled earnestly to justify its existence. As a training school for young officers and soldiers, it rendered valuable aid to the army, and Nicola's letters and reports show a steady flow of recruits through the corps into the field. With the actual invalids matters did not run so smoothly, and at the close of the first year of the corps' existence, Nicola complained that a great many men were lost to the army by the inattention of officers to the orders of Congress. Those men who were transferred drew clothing at the hospitals before starting for the Invalids, sold it on the road, and arrived destitute and had to be clothed again; also because of inattention to detail, they did not bring their pay certificates with them, which resulted in a loss of pay to themselves. Men assigned to the Invalids, but who refused to serve therein, had their names struck off the pension list; but exceptions could be made to this drastic rule by the certification of the governor or president and council of their State in meritorious cases. In September, 1778, Congress made the Pension and Invalid Regulations retroactive so as to include all persons disabled in the military line from the date of the battle of Lexington, thus officially fixing the commencement of hostilities as April 19, 1775.

From the time of its organization until reduced by the action of Congress in 1783, the Invalid Corps proved an organization of value. It performed garrison and guard duty at Philadelphia throughout the war with the single exception of the period when the city was in the possession of the British, and detachments guarded prisoners and stores at Boston, Rutland, Easton, Trenton, and elsewhere. In 1782 General Benjamin Lincoln, then Secretary of War, and unacquainted with the matter, suggested dismissing the corps as a useless expense. Nicola's protest to Washington was blunt and brief:

I can with great propriety [he wrote] assert that, fighting and long marches excepted, no regiment has done more duty besides fatigues; it has now existed upwards of four years . . . and I have heard many officers of marching regiments declare that their men, from seeing the duties and fatigues of the Invalids, dread being transferred. The regiment has not had the honour to attend your Excellency into the field, but has been the means of more serviceable men being called thereto.

A somewhat humorous light is thrown upon the corps in the small riot that occurred in Easton, Pennsylvania, when some of Pulaski's troopers attempted to interfere with a prisoner of the Invalids and were badly beaten up by the men who, though unfit for active field duty, had evidently not forgotten how to fight. This could hardly be wondered at when the record of man after man in the Invalid Corps showed such reason for his presence as wounded at Brandywine, wounded at Monmouth, at Iron Hill, at Yorktown, and other places whose names stand for courage and valor in American army annals.

At the close of the war the corps was concentrated at West Point, and by 1784 it had dwindled down to seven officers and thirty non-commissioned officers and privates. The Commander-in-Chief's feeling for the Invalids is shown in his letter to Baron Steuben of November 8, 1783:

I will request General Lincoln [he wrote], to take measures for having those Invalids who are to go to West Point conveyed thither by water . . . but as General Lincoln is going himself to the Eastward it may require somebody to press the execution of any directions he may send to the

War Office in Philadelphia — and as it is a matter in which humanity is interested I make no apology for requesting you, my dear Sir, to take this upon yourself. With respect to those who cannot be removed or who will ever be incapable of taking care of themselves — let me request you to make the best provision for them you can either by making an agreement for their reception into the Hospital or any other way you may think best — such of them as are entitled to the pension may have their certificates signed as I pass [through] Philadelphia.

Congress had ordered the reduction of the corps in May, 1783; the officers who had lost a limb or been equally disabled were retired on full pay for life; other minor disabilities received half-pay. Disabled non-commissioned officers and privates were to be supported in the hospital for life or they could retire to their homes if they preferred with the same support. All officers and men received a gratuity of one month's full pay on disbanding. The worst cases, seventeen in number, were sent to the Pennsylvania State Hospital; but it was reported that the expectation was for their early recovery and dismissal.

But a year or more before the corps ceased to exist, the general discontent of the army found voice in Nicola's well-known letter to Washington. By 1782 the war was practically over; Cornwallis had surrendered, and only New York, Charleston, and Savannah were held by the British. Both of the Southern cities were evacuated before the year was out and less than a dozen small skirmishes, the last engagements of the war, were fought during the entire twelve months. The mind of the army, freed from thoughts of active campaigning, had time to dwell upon its sufferings and the entire lack of any hopeful sign of improvement. Pay was months in arrears and worth almost nothing when received; supplies were few and everything seemed to be getting worse instead of better. The Invalids' colonel, then a man of sixty-five years, wrote to Washington out of a mind harassed and brooding over the universal gloom and sense of injustice at the neglect which the army was experiencing. His letter and Washington's sharp rebuke are familiar to us, but not so well known is the apology. It is a manly presentation and rings true with no loss of dignity. Nicola wrote two letters to the Commander-in-Chief before he felt that his explanation was complete. It is an apology worthy of record as an example of the manhood of the American Revolution. The first letter follows:

May 23, 1782

Sr.

I am this moment honoured with yours and am extremely unhappy that the liberty I have taken should be so highly disagreeble to your Excellency. Tho I have met with many severe misfortunes nothing has ever affected me so much as your reproof. I flatter myself no man is more desirous to be governed by the dictates of true religion and honour & since I have erred I entreat you will attribute it more to a weakness of judgment than corruptness of heart. No man has entered into the present dispute with more zeal, from a full conviction of the justness of it, & I look on every person who endeavors to disturb the repose of his country as a villain, if individuals disapprove of anything in the form of government they live under they have no other choice but a proper submission or to retire. The scheme I mentioned did not appeal to me in a light anyway injurious to my country, rather likely to prove beneficial, but since I find your sentiments so different from mine I shall consider myself as having been under a strong delusion & beg leave to assure you it shall be my future study to combat, as far as my abilities reach, every gleam of discontent.

Excuse the confusion of this occasioned by the distraction of my mind & permit me to subscribe myself with due respect

Your Excellency's
most obedt. Servant
Lewis Nicola, Col. Inv.

Not satisfied with this, Nicola again wrote to Washington the next day:

May 24, 1782

Sr.

Greatly oppressed in mind and distressed at having been the means of giving your Excellency one moment's uneasiness, I find myself under the necessity of relying on your goodness to pardon my further troubling you by endeavoring, if possible, to remove every unfavorable impression that lies in your breast to my prejudice. Always anxious to stand fair in the opinion of good men the idea of your thinking me capable of acting or abetting any villainy must make me very unhappy.

I solemnly assure your Excellency I have neither been the broacher, or in any shape the encourager of the design not to separate at the peace till all grievances are redressed, but have often heard it mentioned either directly or by hints.

From sundry resolves of Congress favourable to the army, but which that Honble Body has not been able to execute, persons who only see what swims on the surface have laid the blame at their door & therefore lost all confidence in promises, how far this bad impression may affect the larger part of the army I cannot say, but should it operate considerably at the conclusion of the war, it may be expected that all obligations shall be immediately discharged, the posibility of which I much doubt; therefore I took the liberty of mentioning what I thought would be a compromise, bidding fair to be satisfactory to one side and not disadvantageous to the other. Deprived by misfortune of that patrimony I was born to, and, with a numerous family, depending entirely upon my military appointments, when these have failed the tender feelings of a husband and father seeing his family often destitute of the common necessaries of life, have pierced my soul, these feelings often repeated & fraught with anxiety for the future may have sowered my mind & warped my judgment, but in the most sacred manner I protest that had I influence & abilities equal to the task, the idea of occasioning any commotions in a country I lived in would be daggers in my breast and I should think myself accountable at the grand tribunal for all the mischiefs that might ensue. Was it my fate to live under a government I thought insupportable I would look on retiring to some other as the only justifiable means that I could pursue.

As to my opinion on different forms of government, if it be erroneous, I assure you the fault is owing to a defect in judgment not a wilful shutting my eyes to the light of reason.

However wrong the sentiments I have disclosed to your Excellency may be, they cannot have done any mischief, as they have always remained locked up in my breast.

My mind was so disturbed at the perusal of your Excellency's letter that I do not well know what answer I re-

turned, if there was anything improper in it I must trust to
your humanity for pardon & request that you will believe
me with unfeigned respect

Sr

your Excellency's most
obedt Servant

LEWIS NICOLA, Col. Inv.

One year later, in March, 1783, the situation, still
unimproved by Congress, resulted in the dangerous
Newburgh Addresses which required all of Washington's influence and tact to neutralize. With these
anonymous papers Nicola had nothing to do. His
idea was but the substitution of a long tried form of
government for an experimental form that seemed to
be a failure, while the Newburgh Addresses advocated
action that might have developed into a military
despotism, the antithesis of everything for which the
Revolution had been fought.

XII

THE STORY OF THE PURPLE HEART

THE Purple Heart Badge of Military Merit was established by General George Washington in a general order of August 7, 1782, which reads:

The General ever desirous to cherish a virtuous ambition in his soldiers, as well as to foster and encourage every species of Military merit, directs that whenever any singularly meritorous action is performed, the author of it shall be permitted to wear on his facings over the left breast, the figure of a heart in purple cloth or silk, edged with narrow lace or binding. Not only instances of unusual gallantry, but also of extraordinary fidelity and essential Service in any way shall meet with a due reward. Before this favor can be conferred on any man, the particular fact, or facts, on which it is to be grounded must be set forth to the Commander-in-Chief accompanied with certificates from the Commanding officers of the regiment and brigade to which the Candidate for reward belonged, or other incontestable proofs, and upon granting it, the name and regiment of the person with the action so certified are to be enrolled in the book of merit which will be kept at the orderly office. Men who have merited this last distinction to be suffered to pass all guards and sentinels which officers are permitted to do.

The road to glory in a patriot army and a free country is thus open to all — this order is also to have retrospect to the earliest stages of the war, and to be considered as a permanent one.

This was the first time in the history of the United

States Army that an honor badge was provided for the enlisted man in the ranks and the non-commissioned officer, and, though a badge of cloth and sewn on the uniform coat, instead of fastened as a pendent medal, it was, in effect, the medal of honor of the Revolution.

So far as the known surviving records show, this honor badge was granted to only three men, all of them non-commissioned officers: Sergeant Daniel Bissel, of the Second Connecticut Regiment of the Continental Line; Sergeant Daniel Brown, of the Fifth Connecticut Regiment of the Continental Line; and Sergeant Elijah Churchill, of the Second Continental Dragoons, which was also a Connecticut regiment. Connecticut certainly had reason to be proud of her soldiers.

The stories of how the Purple Heart was won by each of these three men can nowhere be found in detail. They can be pieced out from cold official records and by inference, but even in this bare form they should be preserved as a cherished part of the proud record of the old Continental Army.

The first, in point of time, is that of Sergeant Elijah Churchill, of the Second Continental Dragoons. It is in two parts, for it is the story of two raids within the British lines, the first in November, 1780, and the second a year later, in October, 1781. Major Benjamin Tallmadge, of the Second Continental Dragoons, was in charge of the Headquarters secret service, which he managed from the year 1778 to the end of the war, and on November 7, 1780, he received word from his most trustworthy spy that the British had stored several hundred tons of hay, for winter forage, at Coram, Long Island, which is on the north shore, about nine miles southeast from Setauket, or Brookhaven. This forage magazine was protected by a near-by stockade fort, which consisted of three strong blockhouses, connected by a stockade of heavy stakes, twelve feet long and sharpened at the end. There was also a deep ditch, a high wall, and a strong abatis. The work was to mount six cannon, but only two of them were in place when the spy sent in his report. The fortification was called Fort Saint George. The spy's report gave a good description of the work and urged an attempt upon it. Tallmadge, in forwarding the report to Headquarters, volunteered to make the attempt, and Washington, whose prescience in such matters was remarkable, at once gave his permission and left the management of the entire matter to the Major. Tallmadge decided to stake everything on a surprise and formed a party of about fifty of his dismounted dragoons. To take but fifty men across twenty miles of salt water, land them within the enemy's lines, march them at least several miles therein and attempt such a strong fortification as Fort Saint George, might seem to us, at this distance, a reckless and foolhardy thing; but Benjamin Tallmadge, as chief intelligence officer, knew his ground, and, more important than all, knew his troopers. Sergeant Elijah Churchill was one of the men Tallmadge selected. The small detachment marched to Fairfield, Connecticut, nearly opposite to Setauket, Long Island; but there they were delayed eight days by a violent November gale upon the Sound. In the afternoon of November 21st the wind died down. At 4 P.M. the expedition embarked in the whaleboats provided by Lieutenant Caleb Brewster, of Tallmadge's regiment, who had charge of the Continental armed boats on Long Island Sound and who was the conveyer of secret intelligence from the New York and Long Island spies.

The cold blackness of a November night had already settled down when the boats put out from the land, but with wind and oars they crossed in four hours and landed on a deserted stretch of the Long Island shore. They found they had drifted farther from their objective than they expected and a longer march to reach the British fort was now necessary. A large force of British regulars were in winter quarters on Long Island, and there were, in addition, several thousand Loyalist troops, distributed at various points, making it a hazardous venture to march a body of troops for any considerable distance without grave risk of being cut off from their boats. Capture was inevitable if they could not get away from the Island, and the gale that had delayed them on the mainland again swept down upon the Sound. Tallmadge could not risk discovery if his boats could not leave the shore, so he concealed his men in a wood and made the boats as inconspicuous as possible. All day long the men shivered under the forest cover, but, when darkness came again, the wind died down and the cold and stiffened troopers started upon a rapid march down the deserted wintry road. At 3 A.M., November 23d, they were within two miles of Fort Saint George and halted to receive orders for the attack. Tallmadge divided his men into three groups, each of which was to give its entire attention to a specified blockhouse. Sixteen men, in charge of Sergeant Churchill, were to attack the main and largest of the fort buildings. At 4 A.M. the three bodies separated to move against the works from as many different directions. They moved like shadows and with the swiftness of Indians; Churchill and his men were within fifty feet of the fort before the sentinel challenged and fired. Instantly the black winter morning became alive with flame and uproar. Led by the intrepid sergeant, the little party of sixteen plunged through the ditch, swarmed the stockade, and crashed into the fort building before the defenders could settle into organized resistance. The other two attacking parties cleared the defenses almost at the same time and the entire detachment met in the center of the enclosed stockade. But the other parties had expended their energies in getting inside the defenses, and two blockhouses still remained to be taken. A brisk fire was beginning to pour upon the Americans from these two houses, but battering parties beat in the doors and inside of ten more minutes Tallmadge's men had possession of the entire works. The growing light now showed a British supply schooner at anchor close to the shore, near the fort. A detachment captured her with ridiculous ease. The rapidity of the attack had protected the attackers, and they had not lost a man, and only one of them was wounded. The British loss was seven killed and wounded, and most of the latter were mortally hurt. The fort and the schooner were set on fire and the prisoners, over fifty in number, were started back toward the boats under a guard. Leaving a small force to see to it that the fort was completely destroyed, Tallmadge marched with the rest to Coram. The few sentries found there fled, and the hay was pulled loose and set on fire. Over three hundred tons went up in rolling clouds of smoke, and as soon as the fire was going beyond all hope of extinguishment, Tallmadge and his hay-burners started back for the boats. By taking a different road and by rapid marching, they joined the men they had left at Fort Saint George, and overtook the prisoners and their guard inside of two hours. It was now broad daylight and the Loyalist militia were beginning to swarm in their rear. But the two huge columns of smoke, one at Fort Saint George and one at Coram, several miles apart, as well as the unbelievable audacity of a body of rebel troops daring to land on Long

Island, kept the Loyalist militia from approaching too near. They could not believe that only a small party would dare such a thing, and they preferred to wait until their own numbers were sufficient to ensure success against the supposedly large force. By four o'clock in the evening the American party reached the boats, and by this time the British were firing long-range shots at the little column; a small counter-demonstration held the enemy back and the entire force embarked and got away from land without casualties. At 11 P.M., November 23d, they reached Fairfield, having twice crossed Long Island Sound, a total distance of forty miles, marched an equal distance, stormed and taken a fort, destroyed a vessel, the fort, and over three hundred tons of hay, all in less than twenty-four hours.

This was the first exploit in the story of the Purple Heart. The second was Sergeant Churchill's second raid on Long Island, this time against Fort Slongo, which was about forty-eight miles northeast of Brooklyn, on the North Shore. Here the British had built a fort that was a nuisance, and Washington directed Major Tallmadge to look over the ground and report on the advisability of attempting the destruction of the work. The Major immediately slipped over to Long Island to investigate. The risks taken by this brave dragoon officer in establishing and keeping open his channels of spy intelligence to Headquarters were tremendous. The Commander-in-Chief frequently cautioned him and, at times, actually forbade some of his excursions within the British lines. This time Tallmadge returned with drawings of Fort Slongo, exact reports of the British vessels there, their size and strength and the number of troops in the fort and at Lloyd's Neck near by.

With this information he set out for Rhode Island, where the French troops lay, to obtain a naval cooperation from the French fleet. He met and talked with the Comte de Rochambeau and the Chevalier Destouches, but, unfortunately, when he reached Newport, the frigates were out on a cruise and the smaller vessels were scattered. Speed was essential for the success of the plan, so the matter was laid aside. Five months later, when Washington and the main army were in the trenches before Yorktown, Tallmadge made the attempt. This time he formed a force of about one hundred men from the Fifth Connecticut Regiment and the Second Continental Dragoons and sent them over from Compo Point under the command of Major Lemuel Trescott, of the Ninth Massachusetts, who volunteered to manage the raid. Through his spies Tallmadge had such complete information that he knew even the exact spots where the British sentries stood.

The expedition started across the Sound at eight o'clock in the evening of October 2, 1781, and at 3 A.M. of October 3d, the fort was in its hands. Again Sergeant Churchill was in the van of the first attacking party and again he acquitted himself with the utmost gallantry. The fort was so strong that Tallmadge had advised Trescott not to make a direct attack, but to try to draw off the defenders by a feint. This idea was not followed. The attacking force went at their job with such vigor that the fort was taken without the loss of a single man and only four of the British were killed before the works surrendered. The report of the affair shows twenty-one prisoners taken, the destruction of a goodly quantity of artillery and stores of small arms, ammunition, and clothing. It was these two completely successful raids upon fortified works within the enemy's lines on Long Island that gained the Purple Heart for Sergeant Churchill, the award of which was couched in these words:

Sergeant Churchill, of the Second Regiment of Light Dragoons, in the several enterprises against Fort Saint George and Fort Slongo on Long Island, in their [the board of award's] opinion acted a very conspicuous and singularly meritorious part; that at the head of each body of attack he not only acquitted himself with great gallantry, firmness and address, but that the surprise in one instance and the success of the attack in the other, proceeded in a considerable degree from his conduct and management.

The second Heart, awarded to Sergeant Brown, was gained on the historic field of Yorktown. On the evening of October 14, 1781, the two British redoubts that checked the progress of the siege were stormed and taken by the allied troops. The French took the inner, the Americans the outer redoubt, or the one nearest the river. Sergeant Brown led a "forlorn hope," as it is called, because, being the advance party and the first to attack, the hazard is so great that the attackers can have but a forlorn hope of coming through alive. The assault on this British redoubt was under the direction of Lieutenant-Colonel Alexander Hamilton, then serving as a volunteer. Sergeant Brown's party was the first to dash forward, and the brave sergeant did not wait upon the sappers to cut away the abatis and breach the obstacles, but carried his men over all the obstructions and into the redoubt in the face of a murderous fire. The British seem to have been confused by this unethical performance and the redoubt was captured in less than a quarter of an hour, with small loss to the stormers.

The third Purple Heart, which went to Sergeant Bissel, was awarded for an exploit that began in August, 1781, and did not end until September, 1782. In August, 1781, Washington had need of exact and detailed information respecting the British Army in New York City that he was unable to get from his spies, and Sergeant Bissel was sent into the city by Lieutenant-Colonel Robert Hanson Harrison, one of Washington's aides, to obtain it. Though there is no positive evidence of it, it is extremely likely that the plucky sergeant saw and talked with the Commander-in-Chief himself, before he set out upon his hazardous enterprise. He got into the British lines at once, but failed in the main purpose, through no fault of his

own, because he could not get out again. For one long
year he acted the part of a British soldier, in New
York City and on Long and Staten Islands, before he
found means to escape from the latter place. His life
hung by a thread every moment of this time. When
he first entered New York, there was a hot naval press
going on and, to escape being forced into the British
fleet, Bissel enlisted in Benedict Arnold's corps. He
made notes and kept memoranda of troop strengths
and locations and checked his information, one item
against another, until he knew, practically, the exact
situation of the British forces and their condition.
Then the enemy became suspicious of something, and
an order was issued that any soldier found with written information on him would be treated as a spy. To
save his life, Bissel was forced to destroy his precious
memoranda, but he had a good brain and used it to
advantage. When he escaped, in 1782, he went at
once to Headquarters, where he reported to Washington, and his account was written down by Lieutenant-
Colonel David Humphreys. The first four pages of
this report are in Humphreys's handwriting and Bissel, himself, wrote the last three. It is a remarkably
clear statement of facts; what the sergeant knew from
personal observation being distinguished carefully
from what was reported by others and what was mere
hearsay. He described the Staten Island forts and
gave minute descriptions, with sketches, of the forts
on New York and Long Island. The report is endorsed

by Washington himself: "Sergeant Bissel's acct. of the Enemys force and Works at New Yk &c."

These are the exploits of high bravery that gained for three Continental soldiers the Revolutionary medal of honor. Lieutenant-Colonel Jonathan Trumbull, Junior's, first draft of the form of the certificate conferring the Purple Heart upon Sergeant Churchill is endorsed:

Certif for The Badge of Military Merit granted to Sergeant Churchill, 2d Light Dragoons to Serjt. Brown 5th Connct to Serjeant Bissel 2d Con R.

It recites that

it hath ever been an established maxim in the American Service that the Road to Glory was open to All, that Honorary Rewards and Distinctions were the greatest Stimuli to virtuous actions, and that distinguished Merit should not pass unnoticed or unrewarded; and, Whereas, a Board of Officers have reported . . . Now, therefore, Know ye That the aforesaid Sergeant Elijah Churchill, hath fully and truly deserved, and hath been properly invested with the Honorary Badge of Military Merit, and is hereby authorized & intitled to pass and repass all Guards & Military Posts as fully and amply as any Commissioned officer whatsoever; and is hereby further Recommended to that favorable Notice that a Brave and Faithfull Soldier deserves from his Countrymen.

One month after the Purple Heart Badge of Military Merit was established by general orders, on September 9, 1782, another general order directed that:

The Inspector General (or in his absence the inspector of

the Northern Army), the Adjutant General, Brigadier General Huntington, Colonel Greaton and Lieutenant Colonel Barber or any three of them are appointed a Board to examine the pretentions of the non-commissioned officers and soldiers who are candidates for the Badge of Merit — The Board will report their opinion to the Commander-in-Chief. All certificates and recommendations will be lodged with the Adjutant General, who will occasionally summon the Board to assemble.

The only surviving record in the Washington Papers, in the Library of Congress, of the proceedings of such a board, is dated April 24, 1783. This board was composed of Brigadier-General John Greaton, Colonel Walter Stewart, Lieutenant-Colonel Ebenezer Sprout, and Majors Nicholas Fish and Lemuel Trescott. It recommended the award of the Purple Heart to Sergeants Churchill and Brown: to Churchill, in the words quoted previously, and to Brown because "in the assault of the enemy's left redoubt at Yorktown, in Virginia, on the evening of October 14, 1781 [he] conducted a forlorn hope with great bravery, propriety and deliberate firmness and that his general character appears unexceptionable." This choice of staid words on the part of the board holds some unconscious and unintentional humor. It would be interesting to know if the British soldiers defending the redoubt would have thus described the Connecticut sergeant as he came raging over their breastworks at the head of his glittering bayonets.

April 27, 1783, Washington's general orders recited that:

The Board appointed to take into consideration the claims of the Candidates for the Badge of Merit Report: That Serjeant Churchill of the 2d Regiment of Light Dragoons and Serjeant Brown of the late 5th Connecticut Regiment are in their opinion severally entitled to the badge of military merit and do therefore recommend them to His Excellency the Commander-in-Chief, as suitable characters for that honorary distinction. The Commander-in-chief is pleased to order the before named Serjeant Elijah Churchill of the 2d Light Dragoons and Serjeant Brown of the late 5th Connecticut regiment to be each of them invested with the badge of merit. They will call at Head Quarters on the third of May, when the necessary Certificate & Badges will be ready for them.

It is greatly to be regretted that no description of this presentation ceremony has come to light.

The last entry, so far as known, regarding the Purple Heart, is found in Washington's general orders of June 8, 1783, at Newburgh, when Sergeant Bissel was cited for the decoration. It states that:

Serjeant Bissel of the 2d Connecticut regiment having performed some important Services within the immediate knowledge of the Commander-in-Chief, in which the fidelity, perseverance and good Sense of the said Serjeant Bissel were conspicuously manifested; it is therefore ordered that he be honored with the badge of merit; he will call at Head Quarters on tuesday next for the insignia and certificate to which he is hereby entitled.

There were few greater honors possible in the Continental Army than to have General George Washington publicly praise a man for his "fidelity, perseverance and good Sense."

The general orders of this same June 8th also directed that "A Board of officers will assemble at the public Buildings on tuesday at 10 o'clock A.M. to decide upon such pretentions for the badge of merit, as shall be exhibited to them," but no further record has come to light of any awards, other than those to the above three men, of this highest of honors obtained by Continental soldiers.

XIII

PEACE AND DEMOBILIZATION IN 1783

THE peace that ended the Revolutionary War was nearly two years in negotiation. Cornwallis surrendered in October, 1781, and it was not until November 30, 1782, that the Provisional Articles of Peace between Great Britain and the United States were signed at Paris. These Provisional Articles, or, as they are often called, the Preliminary Treaty of Peace, provided that, as agreed upon, they were to be inserted in and to constitute the treaty of peace to be concluded later between Great Britain and the United States, and this definitive treaty was not to be concluded until peace terms were agreed upon between Great Britain and France and, even then, not until His Britannic Majesty was ready to conclude such a treaty. An immediate cessation of all hostilities on land and sea was provided for in these Articles and that all prisoners should be liberated and the British troops and fleets withdrawn from the United States. The wording of these Articles, however, left Great Britain so entirely unhampered that Washington was of the opinion that one more campaign would be necessary before the war ended. An armistice for the mutual cessation of all hostilities was agreed upon and signed by both the British and American commissioners on January 20, 1783, at Versailles.

The first news of this was received from Lafayette, who dispatched a fast-sailing corvette from Spain February 5th, outstripping Benjamin Franklin's official dispatches of January 21st by over two weeks and reaching Congress March 24th, the same day that the Provisional Articles of Peace were received from Sir Guy Carleton, through Washington. The first real peace move in America was taken at once by Congress ordering the recall of all United States armed vessels from the sea. April 10th, Franklin's dispatches arrived and were read in Congress the next day. The proclamation announcing the cessation of hostilities according to the terms of the armistice of January 20th was published by Congress April 11th. Three days later, the release of naval prisoners was ordered and the Commander-in-Chief directed to arrange for releasing all land prisoners. On April 18th, Washington proclaimed in general orders that hostilities on the part of the Continental forces would cease at noon the next day, so that from the signing of the armistice at Versailles to the actual cessation of the war on the sea was exactly two months and five days, and on land, three months, lacking one day. The first gun of the Revolution had been fired April 19, 1775, and hostilities officially ceased by Washington's order April 19, 1783, so that the actual fighting period of the Revolution lasted eight years to the day.

The real treaty of peace, or rather the signatory agreement which made the Preliminary Articles definitive and permanent, was not signed until four months and a half later; but public opinion in America accepted the situation as so conclusive that Congress forced the release of the troops until the army was reduced to skeleton proportions almost at once. Toward the end of May, Alexander Hamilton, then a member of Congress, moved and carried a resolution instructing the Commander-in-Chief to grant furloughs to the non-commissioned officers and soldiers enlisted for the war, who were to be finally discharged as soon as the definitive peace was concluded. Officers, in proportion to the number of men furloughed, were to be released and the Commander-in-Chief and the Secretary of War were to take measures for marching the troops to their respective homes in such manner as would be most convenient to the troops themselves and the States through which they had to pass.

Negotiations in Europe dragged along, but the feeling in America that peace was already an accomplished fact outstripped the fact itself. Had Franklin, Adams, and Jay failed in their negotiation, the resultant situation in the United States is difficult to imagine. Washington moved as directed by Congress, and six months after the signing of the Provisional Articles and four months after the armistice agreement, the first steps were taken toward demobilizing the Continental Army. The first thing done was to prepare returns of the men entitled to furloughs. Soldiers who wished to remain in the service had the privilege of doing so; the officers who were to remain with the army were decided upon by agreement among themselves. The commanders of the various State lines were to make the necessary arrangements to march their commands home, select the routes, and see that the men were properly officered; the contractors who supplied the army were ordered to lay up stores of provisions along the lines of march; the men were permitted to retain their arms and accouterments and the musicians their drums and fifes.

The first troops to march from the Newburgh camp on June 5th were the Marylanders under Major Thomas Lansdale, and his instructions were to proceed along a designated route to Baltimore "in the most easy and convenient manner" for the troops and the inhabitants of the country through which they passed; his instructions concluded:

Relying on your attention to preserve good order and the reputation of your corps, and wishing you and them an agreeable march

    I am, Sir,
     With great esteem,
      Your most humbl Servt
       Go: WASHINGTON

The army was so rapidly reduced by the steady departure of regiments that within a week orders were issued to discontinue the daily parade of all troops except the guards, and in less than two weeks after the

departure of the Maryland battalion the remnant of
the army was ordered to break camp and take station
at West Point; the light troops were formed into a
special corps and moved down into Westchester
County in anticipation of the evacuation of New
York City by the British.

Before the army broke camp at Newburgh, however, the last Badges of Military Merit were be-
stowed upon the non-commissioned officers and privates who had won them by "singularly meritorious
action." This badge consisted of the figure of a heart,
in purple cloth or silk, edged with narrow lace or binding which the soldier wore on his facings over the left
breast. Along with the badge went a certificate signed
by the Commander-in-Chief and the honor man's
name was recorded in a Book of Merit, kept for that
purpose at the orderly office. The conferring of this
honor was announced in general orders and in one case
at least by the Commander-in-Chief's proclamation.
Service stripes were another honor. The men who are
to-day wearing a silver chevron on their left sleeve for
every six months of service in the United States may
feel an additional pride that the ancestry of the insignia traces back to a similar badge of honor in the
Continental Army, and the only difference between
them is the length of service which each stripe repre-
sents and the material of which it is made. In the
Continental Army they were called "honorary badges
of distinction" and were awarded to privates and non-

commissioned officers who had served more than three years "with bravery, fidelity, and good conduct." The badge was "a narrow piece of white cloth of an angular form to be fixed to the left arm of the uniform coat. For six years' service two pieces set on parallel to each other in a similar form." The men thus distinguished were on all occasions "to be treated with particular confidence and consideration."

From June until September matters rested while the news from Europe was awaited with dragging patience. By August, Washington was fairly confident that the war was really over, and on September 19th he wrote to Congress regarding the furloughed men:

On the footing they stand at present a considerable expense without a prospect of an adequate benefit is incurred; unless the impolicy of giving by Public proclamation, while the British forces remain in New York, authenticity to the discharges can be deemed such — I call them discharges because it is in this light the Furloughs have been all along considered, and no call, I am persuaded, will bring the common soldiery back to their Colours — the whole matter therefore lyes in ballancing properly between the expense of delay and the public annunciation at an epoch which may be premature.

One result of this letter was a heated discussion in Congress between those who sought to reduce the federal expenses and those who were opposed to discharging the army while the British forces were still in America. A compromise was reached September 24th when Congress by a secret resolve attempted to put

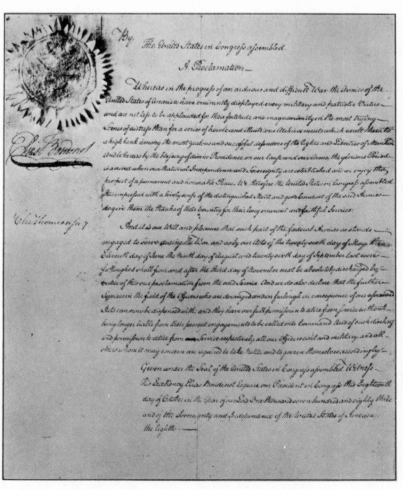

**PROCLAMATION ISSUED BY THE CONGRESS, OCTOBER 18, 1783
DISBANDING THE CONTINENTAL ARMY**

the entire responsibility on the shoulders of Washington by authorizing him to discharge such part of the army as he deemed proper and expedient. Two days later, Congress publicly authorized the furloughing of all general, medical, staff, and engineer officers not needed for the troops in actual service. For nearly a month longer the question of discharging the troops was discussed; finally on October 18th, Congress, "in consequence of a letter from General Washington of September 19, 1783," issued the proclamation disbanding the Continental Army on November 3d. This proclamation, in discharging the troops, gave them "the thanks of their country for their long, eminent, and faithful services."

The troops thus discharged had all reached their homes, and by November 3d the vast majority of them were again absorbed in civil life. November 25th, the British evacuated New York, but it was not until December 13th that news of the signing of the Definitive Treaty of Peace, at Paris, on September 3d, reached Congress. The Definitive Treaty was practically identical in wording with the Preliminary Articles, signed November 30, 1782, and was very short, consisting of only about fifteen hundred words, if the preamble and promulgating paragraph are not counted. It was published by proclamation of Congress January 14, 1784.

The time consumed in negotiating this peace, in which France, Spain, and Holland as well as the

United States were concerned, stretched over two years, for the actual negotiations commenced early in 1782. It took nearly a year to evolve the Preliminary Articles, which were so very contingent as to raise grave doubts of their value to the United States. It took nearly two months to progress from the Preliminary Articles to a cessation of hostilities and over seven months after that to obtain a definite and binding treaty, while if we add to this the time taken for the news to reach America, peace was not officially obtained for over ten months after the fighting ceased.

XIV

A LIBERTY LOAN OF THE REVOLUTION

RECENTLY the paper showing the list of subscribers to a "Liberty Loan" of 1781 was acquired by the Library of Congress. It is a folio-size sheet the clear writing of which shows a total subscription of £1550 sterling, or about $7500 as we reckon pounds sterling to-day. Roughly estimated in dollars, it shows that six of the twenty-four subscribers were $100 men, eight were $250, nine were $500, and one subscribed $650. This paper appears to have been drawn up by the Baltimore Council of Safety as a direction to be followed in obtaining repayment of the loan, for which the Continental Congress assumed the responsibility, though the State of Maryland's willingness to do so is a matter of record. The endorsement describes the paper as the "List of Persons in Baltimore who lent money to the Marquis de la Fayette on Account of the United States."

These were the events that led up to and created the necessity which was met by this loan: In the latter part of the year 1780, Sir Henry Clinton determined to support Cornwallis's campaign in the Carolinas by a demonstration in the Chesapeake Bay region. Benedict Arnold, but lately deserted from the cause of the Colonists, was placed in command. He reached

Hampton Roads the last of December. Counteraction was necessary to prevent Virginia from being overrun, with resultant pressure upon Major-General Greene in the Southern Department, so a detachment of New England troops was formed at Peekskill, New York, and marched to Pompton, New Jersey, where they were joined by certain Jersey troops from Morristown. The Marquis de Lafayette was placed in command of this detachment which was about twelve hundred strong and formed, in part, from the old light infantry that had served under him in the previous campaign. Three weeks after the date of his orders the Marquis and all his troops were under sail in Chesapeake Bay, hoping to take Arnold in the rear while a French squadron from Rhode Island attempted to block the bay entrance. The general plan of the enterprise was not greatly different from that which was successful against Cornwallis a few months later. Unfortunately, the British fleet met and defeated the French off the Virginia Capes, and to save his detachment Lafayette put into Annapolis; Clinton immediately sent a strong reinforcement by sea to Arnold and all chance of an operation against him vanished; Cornwallis was still in the Carolinas and Lafayette's Virginia expedition had failed.

The British made the mistake, however, of sending but two vessels to blockade Annapolis and force Lafayette to make the weary march back to the main army on the Hudson by land. But the young French-

The following sums were advanced the Marquess La Fayette, for which Sums and the Interest, Doctor John Boyd will please to get Bills of Exchange on France from the Hon.ble Rob.t Morris.

1	Sell of Bills drawn in fav.r of			Jacob Hart for	58	19	9
1	d.o	d.o	d.o	d.o	James Calhoun	58	4	5
1	d.o	d.o	d.o	d.o	Richard Curson	50	"	"
1	d.o	d.o	d.o	d.o	James M.cHenry	23	19	7
1	d.o	d.o	d.o	d.o	Nathaniel Smith	20	"	"
1	d.o	d.o	d.o	d.o	John Sterett	53	8	10
1	d.o	d.o	d.o	d.o	Nicholas Rogers	22	"	"
1	d.o	d.o	d.o	d.o	Charles Carroll	25	19	4
1	d.o	d.o	d.o	d.o	Ridley & Pringle	50	"	"
1	d.o	d.o	d.o	d.o	John Smith Jun.r	75	"	"
1	d.o	d.o	d.o	d.o	Stephen Stewart Jun.r	81	"	"
1	d.o	d.o	d.o	d.o	William Smith	100	"	"
1	d.o	d.o	d.o	d.o	William Neill	50	"	"
1	d.o	d.o	d.o	d.o	Alexander Donaldson	25	"	"
1	d.o	d.o	d.o	d.o	Daniel Bowley	50	"	"
1	d.o	d.o	d.o	d.o	Stewart & Salmon	100	"	"
1	d.o	d.o	d.o	d.o	Hugh Young	98	"	"
1	d.o	d.o	d.o	d.o	William Patterson	100	"	"
1	d.o	d.o	d.o	d.o	Sam.l & Rob.t Purviance	100	"	"
1	d.o	d.o	d.o	d.o	John M.cLure	100	"	"
1	d.o	d.o	d.o	d.o	Russell & Hughes	50	"	"
1	d.o	d.o	d.o	d.o	Thomas Russell	45	"	"
1	d.o	d.o	d.o	d.o	Russell & Gilmore	25	"	"
1	d.o	d.o	d.o	d.o	Sam.l Hughes	150	"	"

£ 1550 Sterl.g

The amt. of the Bond ——
The Interest to be added to Each Sum
and included in the Bills

LIST OF SUBSCRIBERS TO " LIBERTY LOAN " OF THE REVOLUTION

man, turned seaman, mounted guns upon two merchant vessels that were in the harbor, swept aside the
blockaders, and sailed his troops in safety back to the
Head of Elk. The necessity of reinforcing Greene
was, however, still existent. The Pennsylvania Continental Line was ordered to prepare for the long
march south and, as Lafayette's detachment was so
much nearer Carolina than any other regular troops,
he was ordered to move overland to Virginia and
there act as circumstances permitted until joined by
the Pennsylvanians. Trouble speedily developed; the
New England troops displayed a spirit of discontent
and objection to Southern service and desertions were
becoming frequent when the Marquis displayed his
genius and understanding of the American character
by placing the matter upon a volunteer basis and
offering to send back any man who did not want to go
and who would apply to him to be relieved. The
trouble ended abruptly, for not a man applied. But
clothing suitable for the South and shoes for the long
march were yet to be obtained. How they were obtained Lafayette tells in his own way in a letter to
Congress dated April 22, 1781, from Alexandria:

I most respectfully beg leave to submit to Congress a
measure which in the present emergency it was necessary
to take, which alone could enable us to follow my instructions and march to the support of the Southern States.

Having no hope of relief from any public magazine, and
being fully convinced that our absolute want of shoes and
linnen put it out of our power to proceed, I have borrowed

from the merchants at Baltimore a sum that (with the addition of a few shoes purchased here) will amount to about two thousand guineas — for this I became a security and promised it would be returned with the interests in two years' time, engaging, however, to make exertions for an earlier payment. Should Congress be pleased to leave to me the management of this affair, I will propose that the Government of France have this money added to any loan Congress may have procured in that Country, and will also endeavor to reduce the debt of Congress to the primitive sum for which these articles have been bought in France.

This measure which want of time obliged me to take upon myself, and which I beg Congress will please to excuse may enable me to furnish every non-commissioned officer and soldier in the detachment with one shirt and one pair of over-alls — some hats and some shoes will also be procured. I am under great obligations to the merchants of Baltimore for their readiness to afford me their succour, and feel myself particularly indebted to the ladies of that town who have been pleased to undertake the making up of the shirts for our detachment.

The several articles mentioned in this letter were of an immediate necessity — but we do greatly want a succour from the Board of War. Our circumstances are peculiar — our clothing more ragged than usual. . . . Both officers and soldiers have an indefatigable zeal — but I think it my duty the more warmly to expose their wants as their fortitude and virtue patiently and cheerfully carries them through every kind of hardship. . . .

Here is a familiar parallel to our situation in 1918: the need of haste in furnishing supplies, the Liberty Loan subscribers, the splendid work of our women volunteers, and the steady courage of our soldiers. In replying to Lafayette's letter, the President of Congress wrote on May 28th:

It is with pleasure & satisfaction that I obey the directions of Congress in transmitting the enclosed resolve of the 24th instant and assuring you, Sir, that they will take proper measures to discharge the engagements you have so generously entered into with the merchants of Baltimore to obtain supplies for the detachment under your command. This is but one instance among the many proofs you have given of your zeal and attachment to the interests of these United States. . . .

Of the zeal and attachment of this son of France to the cause of Liberty no other evidence is needed than this pledge of his private fortune for a loan that was to bring freedom to America by equipping her troops for the final struggle. To-day (1918), one hundred and thirty-seven years later, America is pledging her entire fortune to stand shoulder to shoulder with the country of Lafayette in a struggle for the freedom of the world.

And we know no more of the end to-day than did those two dozen patriots of 1781; they knew only that a detachment of their gallant army needed supplies that their money could furnish. They did not know that their subscriptions would make possible a troop movement that was to win the war. Actuated only by a desire to "do their bit," they performed a service to America worthy of lasting record, for the struggle begun on the village green at Lexington was marked to end in the battered trenches of Yorktown when Lafayette's detachment, clothed and shod by this loan, swung out of Baltimore on its march south. Is it more than a coincidence that this march commenced on April 19th? By rapid movement the troops reached Richmond only a few hours before the British appeared on the south bank of the James and then began the series of maneuvers that led Cornwallis, before the summer was over, into the fatal trap at Yorktown. The Liberty Loan of 1781 had done its bit!

XV

A SEA CAPTAIN OF THE REVOLUTION

THIS is the story of Andrew Paton, captain of the
good ship *Lady Margareta* which sailed from Cadiz,
Spain, for Edenton, North Carolina, in the winter of
1777–78 with a miscellaneous cargo of supplies.

On an extra-large sheet of thin, handmade, linen
paper, Captain Paton gives the facts, in a blunt, sea-
manlike fashion, of his encounter with a British
man-o'-war and the British Court of Admiralty in
New York; his imprisonment on a British prison-ship
in New York Harbor and his daring escape therefrom.
The narrative came to light but recently, among a
mass of papers with which no connecting link is apparent, and, as a picture of a Revolutionary War
adventure, it is unique. A succession of thrilling
incidents is set down in the most matter-of-fact
way, beginning with the opening sentences in quaint
chirography and still quainter spelling:

In Seven days after my departor from Cadez, I made the
Islands of Porto, Santo & Madera, the wind to the N/ward
& westward, I steared to the Suthard untill I goot in the
Latitid. 30° ″00. Continued Running down my Longd. In
the Parrell, until I goot in the Longd. of 65° ″00 west.

Here he met with heavy gales and contrary winds
which drove the ship about on the coast of America

and prevented his making a port. With him, as a passenger, was a Dutch sea captain and his wife, and, with the aid of this complacent and phlegmatic Hollander, Paton was able, later, to puzzle the British so successfully as to save his ship from confiscation.

For days Paton strove to make safe harbor in the face of heavy offshore gales, but with no success; then the storm subsided and, with clearing weather, the inevitable happened! On January 14, 1778, a sail appeared to the northward and bore swiftly down upon him. Anxiously Paton studied the stranger through his spyglass and finally made her out to be a British man-o'-war. Instantly he hoisted the Dutch flag and, diving below, hastily swept together his private journal and all his papers relating to America, bundled them into a tight packet and cannily dropped them overboard unnoticed by the pursuing ship. Only the log-book and manifests were left, and these contained no incriminating information that would show that Paton was an American. In less than an hour the pursuing ship came within range and dropped a round shot with a whistling splash along the forefoot of the *Lady Margareta*. Paton promptly hove to with the Dutch flag flapping at the mizzen. Down came the man-o'-war and ran up into the wind under the *Lady Margareta's* stern.

"What ship is that?" bawled a hoarse voice through a speaking trumpet.

Paton had his answer ready. Luckily he was, at the

time he was sighted, standing to the southward and a safe neutral port in that direction was the island of Curaçao, off the coast of Dutch Guiana.

"The Dutch ship *Lady Margareta*, from Cadiz to Curaçao, sixty-nine days out," was his answer.

A pause ensued and then the order came: "Come aboard, you."

Paton ordered out his gig and he and the Dutch captain, together with the non-committal log-book, were rowed over to the man-o'-war. On the way he rapidly coached the Hollander to claim to be the captain of the *Lady Margareta*. The man-o'-war proved to be the British ship *Experiment*, Sir James Wallace, captain, and he put the two men through a rigorous cross-examination.

From Paton he extracted no information, as that clever seaman declared himself to be merely a passenger who knew next to nothing about the sea or ships and was only concerned about reaching his destination. From the Dutch captain there was even less to be learned. The phlegmatic Hollander blinked owlishly, bluntly objected to the examination, protested against having been stopped, and then relapsed into a stolid silence that exasperated the British commander. In a rage at finding himself balked in taking what looked like a valuable prize, Sir James declared the *Lady Margareta* a suspicious vessel and announced his determination to convoy her into New York for examination. A prize crew of two officers and twelve men were put on board the *Lady Margareta*, and Captain Paton and eleven of his crew transferred to the *Experiment* and the two vessels proceeded to New York. The merchantman ran up the harbor to the city; but the man-o'-war, with Captain Paton on board, anchored at Sandy Hook.

Up in the city the Dutch captain, the mate of the *Lady Margareta*, and most of the crew were examined before the British Court of Admiralty; but as only the Hollander, his wife, and Paton knew whither the ship had been bound, the amount of dependable information obtained was small and, as Paton described it: "All turning out to Nothing in Regard of Condemning ye ship & Cargo."

How successfully Paton's strategy worked is attested by the newspaper report of the arrival which described the *Lady Margareta* as a prize ship of six hundred tons, commanded by Captain De Ruyter, with a large and valuable cargo of salt, medicines, between four and five thousand weight of Jesuit's bark (as quinine was then known), wine, brandy, cordage, linens, tea, and mercery goods, bound from Cadiz to Curaçao, but whose destination was suspected as South Carolina. The estimated value of the cargo was eighty-four thousand dollars, and it was called a fine prize for Captain Wallace and his men.

Disgusted with the failure to libel successfully the *Lady Margareta* on the information obtained from De Ruyter, Captain Paton was next brought up from

Sandy Hook and called before an examining board on His Majesty's Ship *Preston*. The British naval officers were puzzled and irritated at the slight headway they were making against a wall of dead resistance. They were convinced that something was wrong, but were unable to put their hands upon the difficulty. When Paton entered the cabin of the *Preston*, they attempted to carry off the proceedings in a high-handed manner. A puffy, important-looking officer at the head of the table conducted the questioning.

"You are a seaman — don't deny it, sir!" he barked accusingly at Paton.

"In a manner of speaking, no," was Paton's answer. "But I have sailed the seas somewhat as a passenger, as I was doing this time."

"You have all the appearance of a seafaring man, and you talk like one," was the next accusation.

"Mayhap I have and mayhap I do," answered Paton coolly. "It would go hard if I did not learn some of the manners of the sea by having sailed with many different masters and by being examined, too, by such a board of officers as this."

"You are insolent, sir!" growled the officer.

"No," answered Paton easily, "I haven't a chance to be."

Seeing nothing was to be gained on this tack, the next question was a more direct charge.

"How was it that though you are not a seaman you helped Captain De Ruyter navigate the ship?"

This was a poser, for Paton did not know just what they had found out from De Ruyter; however, least said soonest mended, so he stuck to his plan of ignorance and answered:

"I don't know navigation, but I know enough to follow directions," he protested. "Whatever I did was to oblige Captain De Ruyter."

"We'd best lock up this fellow," said the examining officer, "and have the Dutchman sent in again to-morrow."

So off Paton was sent, but he cleverly managed, through one of the crew, to get word to De Ruyter to make out a protest against Captain Wallace and the *Experiment* for the seizure, to swear it out before a justice of the peace; to stick to the sworn statement, refuse to say a word more, and on no account to submit to a second examination. De Ruyter followed out this programme to the letter. This blocked the proceedings and the protest, together with De Ruyter's refusal again to appear before the examining board, prevented the second examination.

The British authorities were in a quandary. Until they could prove their case against the *Lady Margareta*, they dared not go beyond the point they had reached for fear of a damage claim through their High Mightinesses, the States General of the United Netherlands; yet they could not hope to seize the ship without resorting to measures that would most likely involve them with the Dutch Government, which was already sympathetic toward America.

All hope of legally condemning the *Lady Margareta* had vanished; but one last chance remained. Paton was not a citizen of Holland, that much was sure, so they could venture a little pressure upon him. He was dragged before the Court of Admiralty and subjected to a grilling examination for five long hours; but again the British failed to trap the wary seaman, and, as Paton states:

All that not being sattesfaction enuf to the Enemeys of America & they finding nothing that they could condemn the Ship upon, I was ordered to be sent on board one of the Prison ships at N. York, thinking at the same time that my hard Confinement would make me confess the Destination of the ship so as to obtain my liberty & the Bribes that was offered me.

It was here that Paton showed his nerve and courage still more plainly. "After that," he writes, "I found that there was no such thing as to Obtain my Liberty by fair means, so I was determined to have it by fowll." He was a rapid worker, and his "fowll" means consisted of forming a plan with three of the American prisoners on board who had not been on the ship long enough to have lost either their nerve or their strength. On the seventh night of Paton's imprisonment their plans were ready. Paton had not been searched and he had with him a goodly quantity of "Dutch courage" in the shape of a flask of rum. Not being a military prisoner he had, it seemed, a certain amount of freedom on board the prison-ship, so, as night came on, he made friendly advances to the two deck sentries; probably an easy thing to do when the friendship was escorted by warming nips from his flask. After darkness set in, Paton succeeded in maneuvering his three conspirators on deck and the four Americans proceeded to get both sentries expeditiously and completely drunk. Their next move was to hoist the deck boat over the bulwarks and lower her down into the water. To a clever seaman this was easy, and by good luck neither fall nor tackle creaked. Paton's next act was characterized by a certain grim humor mixed with practical common sense, for he caused the drunken sentries to be carefully lowered into the boat. This not only effectually prevented them from giving the alarm, but made them partners to the escape. They pushed off quietly from the prison-ship and managed to make the Long Island shore before daybreak without being detected by the guard boats. Landing, they pushed the boat adrift with its freight of drunken sentries and set off inland; they soon separated for greater safety and each man struck out for himself.

The next night Paton boldly crossed the ferry into New York City, where he found an American sympathizer and remained in hiding in the man's house for a week. During that time he succeeded in getting word to De Ruyter and the two met for several nights, when Paton gave him full and complete instructions how to act regarding the *Lady Margareta* and her cargo. These were to take the ship out of New York

Harbor, bound for Curaçao as soon as the British gave her up as hopeless; but, when well clear of New York, to run for the nearest Southern port in the United States, if possible; barring that he was to throw the ship, if he could, into the hands of one of the American cruisers, as a prize. After this was thoroughly understood, Paton confesses, naïvely, that he "was afrid to remain aney Longer amongst my Enemeys," so he crossed again to Long Island and, traveling by night, finally reached the extreme east end and crossed over to New London.

His narrative was written when he reached Boston, a few days later, and is dated at that city May 6, 1778. It is the blunt effort of a good seaman and an honest man to explain the loss of his ship. He finishes his recital thus: "The Dutch Capt., when I left New York, together with his Peapel, was Still remaining in Posesing of Ship & Cargo." And he adds a formal touch with this legal flourish: "To All Whom this may Consern. Witness my hand, ANDW. PATON."

That the loss of the *Lady Margareta* did not injure Paton's reputation as an able seaman is attested by the fact that three years afterwards he sailed for Hispaniola in the new-built merchant ship *Betsey*, owned by the firm of Nelson & Fox, of Philadelphia.

The *Betsey* carried a crew of forty men and was armed with ten six-pounders. With these guns and with Captain Paton in command of her, it may well be doubted that she was ever captured by the British.

XVI

THE "UNITED STATES OF AMERICA"
AND THE "U.S.A."

EVERY one, of course, is familiar with the genesis of
the name of our country and can point to the official
adoption of the title "United States" by the Continental Congress; but not every one knows that the
abbreviation "U.S.A." has an equal sanction in law
and was not born of our national habit of taking slang
short cuts. "U.S." for United States seems to have no
authority beyond this national habit, but "U.S.A."
was officially selected and its story is not uninterest-
ing, interwoven as it is with the more familiar one of
the selection of the name "United States."

The germ idea in the title "United States" is found,
of course, in the birth of the idea of a union of the
Colonies, and Benjamin Franklin may quite properly
be given the honor of being its godfather. At the time
of the Albany Congress, in which he played so promi-
nent a part, and a decade before the Stamp Act troubles, his "Pennsylvania Gazette" typified the necessity of union by the diagram of a dissevered snake
with its pieces named for the Colonies and the whole
bearing the pregnant warning: "Unite or Die." This
diagram, which was probably the earliest American
newspaper political cartoon, was redrawn and ap-

peared again in Massachusetts, New York, and Pennsylvania newspapers in 1774 and played its part in popularizing the union or united idea in the public mind. Union became a fact with the assembling of the First Continental Congress in that year, but the word or idea of union or united Colonies did not appear in any of its proceedings.

The Second Continental Congress convened May 10, 1775, in response to the recommendation of the First, and the word "united" appears in its proceedings for the first time on June 7, 1775, when it was resolved that July 20th be observed "throughout the twelve United Colonies" as a day of humiliation, fasting, and prayer. The quoted words are not in the original journals of the proceedings of the Congress, but were added later, by Charles Thomson, the Secretary of Congress, in the so-called corrected journal. The first draft of this recommendation to the Colonies to observe a day of humiliation does not, curiously enough, contain the word "united." It is interesting to note that the first official public use of the word "united" occurs in the draft of the commission to the Commander-in-Chief of its armies, June 17, 1775, which begins: "The delegates of the United Colonies of New Hampshire, Massachusetts Bay, etc., to George Washington, Esquire," and in the instructions of Congress to the new Commander-in-Chief occurs the phrase "the good people of the united colonies."

From then on the term "United Colonies" was used until the adoption of the Declaration of Independence. The committee to whom was entrusted the drafting of that immortal document brought in its report June 28, 1776, with the caption title "A Declaration by the Representatives of the United States of America in General Congress Assembled." This heading was changed in the Declaration, as adopted July 4th, to "The unanimous Declaration of the thirteen United States of America." The "United States" appears again in the proceedings of Congress of July 8th in granting General Washington permission to engage the St. Johns and other Indians in the service. The next occasion of its appearance was in the draft of the Articles of Confederation which was reported July 12th, the first article of which read: "The name of this Confederacy shall be 'The United States of America.'" The Articles of Confederation were not finally adopted until 1781, but article 1 was adopted in practice from July, 1776. Drafts of State papers considered by the Congress from then on quite frequently abbreviated this title to the "U. States," rarely to "U.S.," and the formal completed instrument always gave in full "the" or "these United States of America." On September 9, 1776, Congress resolved that in all Continental commissions and other instruments where, theretofore, the words "United Colonies" had been used the style be altered for the future to "United States."

The abbreviation "U.S.A.," curiously enough, had its beginning in poor quality gunpowder. June 7, 1776, two weeks before the draft of the Declaration of Independence was reported, Henry Wisner, Robert Treat Paine, and Robert R. Livingston were appointed a committee to inquire into the defect of the gunpowder manufactured at Oswall Eve's mill at Frankfort, Pennsylvania, and instructed to take measures to remedy it. They submitted their report August 28, 1776, and according to their recommendations, Congress resolved that inspectors be appointed to judge the quality of all gunpowder. Every caskful manufactured or purchased was to be examined and none received into the public magazines for the use of the United States of America but such as had been approved by the public inspector as to its quickness in firing, strength, dryness and other necessary qualities. The inspector was to mark each cask so approved with the letters "U.S.A." and such other marks as were necessary to distinguish the several sorts of powder. Robert Towers was elected by Congress the first inspector of gunpowder.

This was the first official determination to use a distinguishing mark or brand, and it is difficult to understand why, in the matter of marking other Continental property, arms, accouterments, etc., this convenient and unmistakable letter triad was not settled upon. Instead, however, the Congress went back to the full words "United States." The necessity of branding or marking firearms became plain before the year 1776 had more than started, and February 16th, Washington's general order to the troops besieging Boston directed the colonels of the various regiments to have the arms branded with the number of the regiment or stamped and marked in such a manner as to prevent their theft and sale, a common practice. A year later the Continental Board of War advised Congress to issue a circular letter to the States setting forth the necessity of putting a strong army in the field and that the most effectual steps be taken for collecting from the inhabitants, not in actual services, all Continental arms, and to give notice of the number they shall collect to General Washington. That all arms or accouterments belonging to the United States be stamped or marked with the words "United States"; that all arms already made be stamped on such parts as would receive the impression and that those hereafter manufactured be stamped with those words on every part composing the stand; all arms and accouterments so stamped or marked were to be seized wherever found unless they should be in the hands of those actually in the Continental service.

The difficulties of the situation are shown in a letter from Washington to Lieutenant-Colonel Benjamin Flower, the Commissary of Artillery at Philadelphia, under date of March 31, 1777:

The great waste and embezzlement of public arms and the difficulties arising from thence make it necessary that the utmost precautions should be used to restrain such infamous practices and future losses. I know no way so likely to effect it as that of putting on them some mark indicating them to be public property, and therefore request that you will have all belonging to the States, as well as those which have been lately imported, as all others as far as circumstances will permit of, stamped with the words *"United States"* on such parts as will receive the impression, which designation should be also put on all their accoutrements. This Congress determined to be done by a Resolve of the 24th ulto. and if they have not, it is so essential that it could not be dispensed with. As there are and will be many public arms here which ought to be secured by the same impression I wish you to have several stamps made and sent by the earliest opportunity to Mr. French, Commissary of Stores here with directions to advise me of their arrival that they may be immediately used.

The resolve of Congress of February 24th adopted, almost verbatim, the recommendations of the Board of War advising the marking of arms as given above and, in addition, suggested that the States pass laws providing for the punishment of all who should withhold, secrete, or steal public arms. The difficulty continued, and on April 12, 1777, Brigadier-General Alexander McDougall wrote to Washington from Peekskill, New York:

The loss of Public Arms through the neglect of Officers and the wickedness of the Men and the plunder of Citizens, calls for some expedient to designate them, in order that they may be discovered and taken. The want of this enabled many of the men to carry off some of our best Arms under the pretense of being their Own. To prevent these evils, there should be a Brand with some device on it,

expressive of the Public property, with which the arms of
the Continent should be branded; and to this may be
added a Stamp capable of making an impression by a
stroke on the barrel, and a number of these should be at
every Post to Brand and Stamp all the Continental Arms.
A number might soon be made at Boston or Philadelphia.
This being done it wou'd not be easy for Villains to rob the
Public. We could then seize the Arms wherever we find
them. As I understand we have had an arrival lately of
many new Arms, some means should be devis'd to secure
them for the Continent against plunderers.

Washington's effort to meet the situation is shown
in his reply, April 17th:

It is really difficult to say what has become of our Arms
— It is certain we had many & such as were valuable in
their quality — In store there are but few. Nor are they to
be found in the different States; at least the applications
from the Eastward are most pressing upon this subject.
To prevent future embezzlements the Congress have resolved that all belonging to the Public, with their accoutrements, shall be stamped with the words *United States*, and
that they shall be seizable wheresoever they are afterwards
found. I wish you to procure Stamps that those of the
States in the Regiments with you, may receive the impression — I have directed some to be brought from Philadelphia part of which I will order to be sent to you if you
can't procure them elsewhere.

On April 18, 1777, Washington issued a general
order from Morristown:

All the Continental Arms, those in possession of the
troops, as well as those in Store, to be marked immediately.
Commanding Officers of Corps to see this Order put in
execution — they will get the Brand by applying to the
Commissary of Military stores.

To Brigadier-General Samuel Holden Parsons he wrote on April 23d:

As to arming the drafts, if they have not arms of their own and the State cannot furnish them they must be supplied with those belonging to the Public. But I must observe that you cannot be too careful in taking proper and most exact accounts of all your deliveries and to what officers. And to prevent in future the scandalous abuses arising from embezzlement & other causes all arms under the latter denomination with their accoutrements are to be stamped with the words *United States* on the barrel and such places as will receive the impression. This is by a Resolve of Congress & being founded in the most evident necessity, must be minutely attended to.

One more difficulty was to be solved before the matter of identification of public property was settled. McDougall encountered opposition from the Massachusetts troops when he started to stamp their arms, for they maintained that their firelocks were their own personal property inasmuch as the State had forced them to pay for them when they entered the service. Washington's settlement of the tangle was swift and conclusive. In answer to McDougall's report he wrote, May 7, 1777:

By what rule or by what right the State of Massachusetts undertook to make their soldiers pay for the public arms, I cannot conceive. To give the soldier the least pretense to a property in his arms, except so far as to pay for them if he lost or destroyed them, was what I had been labouring to put a stop to: But to admit this would be to put things upon the same bad footing which they had been. I therefore desire that all the arms & accoutrements without exception, may be branded, and if anything has been stopped from the soldiers, for their arms, I will order it to be returned.

From this time on no signs of trouble in the marking of arms appear, and we may conclude that the brand "United States" performed its full duty.

Growing out of the necessity for political union to obtain economic and political justice, the name of our country rests in the draft of the Declaration of Independence — the joint approval of that committee of the Continental Congress consisting of Thomas Jefferson, John Adams, Benjamin Franklin, Roger Sherman, and Robert R. Livingston. The symbol "U.S.A." was officially adopted and used as a distinguishing label before the words "United States" were so used. It rests in the joint authorship of Henry Wisner, Robert Treat Paine, and Robert R. Livingston; and, where "United States" was used to mark the arms with which our political and economic independence was obtained, "U.S.A." was a guarantee for the powder, in the absence of which those arms would have been useless.

XVII

THE POST-OFFICE OF THE REVOLUTIONARY WAR

THE Post-Office of the United States, as a distinct civic establishment, is built upon a foundation supplied by the energy and enterprise of an American newspaper publisher. A year or more before the outbreak of the Revolutionary War it came into existence in opposition to the Royal Mail Service in the Colonies and reached such a point of efficiency that, when the Continental Congress established a postal service, it meant little more than taking over and systematizing William Goddard's newspaper mail.

The Royal Mail in the Colonies became a source of irritation to the people with the beginning of the Stamp Act excitement. The postal rates were high and the business methods a mixture of arrogance and superciliousness. When the struggle against the Crown commenced, the Royal Post-Office interfered in every possible way that could block the efforts of the Colonies to obtain unanimity of action. It delayed and suppressed news and mishandled mail. Letters were opened, read, and destroyed, and the information thus obtained was transmitted to the royal authorities. Such interference was serious, and this and many petty tyrannies of the Post were decided factors in rousing the spirit of protest and rebellion, especially among the business and mercantile classes.

William Goddard was the owner and publisher of the "Maryland Journal and Baltimore Advertiser," a weekly newspaper that espoused the cause of the Colonies with fearless enthusiasm. Because of its pungent criticism of British administrative measures, his paper was practically barred from the mail a year or more before the war began. With true American newspaper enterprise, Goddard refused to be balked, and forthwith established a line of riders from Massachusetts to Georgia. These post-riders, almost at once, were entrusted with carrying small parcels and letters by the people along the routes, as their service was regular and more dependable than that of the Royal Mail riders. By August, 1774, Goddard's service was in full operation and the revenues of the Royal Mail were seriously curtailed by the competition. It was not a peaceful competition, however, and there were frequent personal encounters and much bad blood displayed by the competing riders when they chanced to meet upon the road. These were, in effect, the preliminary skirmishes of the war that was soon to break forth.

A month after Lexington, the Continental Congress appointed a committee, of Benjamin Franklin, who had been the Deputy Postmaster-General of the Royal Mail in the Colonies; Thomas Lynch; Richard Henry Lee, who later introduced the resolution of Independence; Thomas Willing; Samuel Adams, and

Philip Livingston, to consider the best means of establishing posts for conveying letters throughout the continent, as the then critical situation rendered it highly necessary that ways and means be devised for the speedy and sure conveyance of intelligence from one end of the Colonies to the other. This committee brought in a report, July 25, 1775, which was considered and adopted the next day, so that the Post-Office, which came into existence by the adoption of this report, was the second executive department created by the Continental Congress. The first, naturally enough in a frontier country, was the Indian Department. As established, the Post-Office consisted of a Postmaster-General of the United Colonies, whose office was to be in Philadelphia; a Secretary, a Comptroller or Auditor, and the necessary number of deputies, or postmasters, in charge of the post-offices throughout the Colonies. The post-riders, or mail-carriers, were looked upon, apparently, as mere messengers, or employees, and were not given much consideration, then or later, though, had it not been for their services, the rest of the organization would have fallen to the ground as useless. The main or trunk line of post-offices reached from Falmouth, now Maine, to Savannah, Georgia, with cross-lines to the interior as needed. The Postmaster-General's salary allowance at the start was one thousand dollars, and the postmasters were allowed, in lieu of salary, twenty per cent of all postage paid into the office when the whole amount was under one thousand dollars a year, and ten per cent when the amount exceeded one thousand dollars. The postage rates were established at twenty per cent less than those of the Royal Mail, which had been one shilling eight pence on single letters (letters written on one sheet of paper only), not carried over sixty miles; two shillings when carried one hundred and two hundred miles; three shillings eight pence for between two hundred and three hundred miles; four shillings for between three hundred and four hundred miles, and four shillings six pence for between four hundred and five hundred miles. The rate was doubled for double letters (letters written on two sheets of paper), treble for treble letters, and so on; the postage on an ounce package equaled that of four single letters.

Congress pledged itself to supply any money deficiency and elected Benjamin Franklin the first Postmaster-General. Franklin immediately appointed William Goddard as his Surveyor-General of Post-Roads, which was the same as supervisor of post-riders, and Richard Bache, his Secretary and Comptroller. This was the modest beginning of the official Post-Office Department of the United States, and these three men put into operation the postal system which has continued, without a break, down to the present and ranks to-day with the United States Treasury in importance to the well-being of the Nation.

The complete Post-Office establishment included,

of course, the postmasters. Unfortunately, no full record of these has survived; but it is possible to check up a nearly complete list of the postmasters and post-offices from 1775 through 1777, and these will be here given because it has nowhere been published before and because these men contributed a valuable share of the combined effort that gained our independence.

The main line of the mail ran north and south from Philadelphia, the central office. Northward the stages were: Philadelphia to Easton, Pennsylvania; Easton to Fishkill, New York; Fishkill to Hartford, Connecticut; Hartford to Boston; Boston to Portsmouth, New Hampshire; and Portsmouth to Falmouth (then in Massachusetts, now in Maine). To the south the line ran: Philadelphia to Annapolis, Maryland; Annapolis to Williamsburg, Virginia; Williamsburg to Halifax, North Carolina; Halifax to Wilmington in the same State; Wilmington to Charleston, South Carolina; and Charleston to Savannah, Georgia. There were deputies in each of the above main-station post-offices and intermediate stations were established as needed. The mail passed twice a week to each of the main stations and the postal regulations demanded one hundred miles of travel from the post-riders every twenty-four hours, even though this might mean riding both day and night. The riders were paid twelve pence Pennsylvania currency per mile from October 20th to April 20th, and eight pence per mile from April 20th to October 20th. While the army was at

Cambridge, during the siege of Boston, the riding stages between Philadelphia and Washington's Headquarters were Brunswick, New Jersey; Dobbs Ferry on the Hudson; Fairfield, Hartford, Woodstock, and Cambridge.

The year 1775 passed with the civil organization of the Revolutionary Government shaking down into place. Despite the many and heavy demands on Franklin's time, he succeeded in systematizing and improving the mail service to such an extent that by the end of 1776, when he gave up the Postmaster-Generalship to become United States Commissioner to France, the postal service was running with comparative smoothness and commendable efficiency. In 1776 the franking of mail, free postage of official letters, was introduced. It did not come into existence without a struggle, for the men of the Revolution were chary and suspicious of anything savoring of special privilege. They had seen the evils of political favoritism and it was largely because of such evils that they had been driven to rebel against their king. The privilege was first proposed for the soldiers in the field, and, after considering the matter for two weeks, Congress granted free postage to the troops actually engaged in active service; later this privilege was extended to the officers, and toward the end of the year to the Board of War. The Commander-in-Chief and the President of Congress had the privilege from the beginning.

Postmasters were exempt from military service and the post-riders were likewise excused, these last by a resolve of August 8, 1776. At the end of August, Congress formulated additional regulations which provided a post-rider for every twenty-five or thirty miles of mail route, and each rider was expected to cover his stage three times a week, setting out immediately on receipt of mail and traveling without stops to the next rider. This was the pony-express plan that was so successfully operated in the Far West a century later, and it is interesting to know that our Continental Congress planned a service that was developed to its highest point of efficiency by the Western plainsman, William F. Cody, better known as "Buffalo Bill," one hundred years afterwards. A trouble in 1776 was keeping the riders up to their schedule, a point in the later Western pony express that was taken care of by the personal pride of the plainsman in his reputation as a hard rider. But this pride was non-existent in 1776, and Congress suggested that the Postmaster-General institute a system of waybills or some similar check method to prevent the delay on the part of the post-riders. In these additional regulations of August, Congress provided for three mail or "advice" boats, to ply between North Carolina, South Carolina, Georgia, and the nearest port to the seat of Congress. These boats were to be armed, and the frugal-mindedness of the Congress was displayed in the proviso that the boats carry cargoes, to meet the expense of their operation.

A record of the Post-Office personnel for the first years of the Revolution does not seem to have survived. It is doubtful if one for 1775 was ever specifically compiled; but from 1776 up to 1778 we have what appears to be a nearly complete record, and it is from this record that the following names are given, as a roster of civilian patriots deserving a place on the honor roll of the Revolution: Falmouth (Maine), Samuel Freeman and Moses Swift, postmasters; Portsmouth, New Hampshire, Samuel Penhallow and Jeremiah Libbey; Salem, Massachusetts, Edward Norris and Mascoll Williams; Newburyport, Massachusetts, Bulkley Emerson; Ipswich, Massachusetts, Daniel Noyes; Middletown, Massachusetts, Hobby Winsley; Springfield, Massachusetts, Moses Church; Fairfield, Connecticut, Thaddeus Burr; Stratford, Connecticut, Ebenezer Weed; Hartford, Connecticut, William Ellery, Thomas Hilldrup, and J. Hastings; New Haven, Elias Beers, G. Saltonstall; Westerly, Rhode Island, Joel Babcock and —— Goddard; Newport, Rhode Island, Solomon Southwick; Greenwich, Rhode Island, G. Mumford; Providence, Rhode Island, John Carter; Fishkill, New York, Samuel Loudoun; Fredericksburg, New York, William Smith and James Taylor; Little Rest, New York, William Potter; Trenton, New Jersey, Abraham Hunt and James Paxton; Princeton, New Jersey, Hugh Montgomery; Elizabethtown, New Jersey, Edward Thomas and

Cochran Prider; Morristown, New Jersey, Frederick King; Bristol, Pennsylvania, Charles Bessonet; Easton, Pennsylvania, Robert Trail; Reading, Pennsylvania, Henry Haller; Philadelphia, Peter Baynton, who was also Comptroller of the Post-Office; Susquehanna, Pennsylvania, John Rogers; Wilmington, Delaware, Jacob Broome; Newcastle, Delaware, Mrs. Clay; Head of Elk, Maryland, Jacob Hollingsworth and Joseph Stiles; Baltimore, Maryland, Mary K. Goddard; Annapolis, Maryland, William Whitcroft and William Goldsmith; Bladensburg, Maryland, Christopher Lowndes; Upper Marlboro, Maryland, Stephen West; Georgetown, Maryland, Thomas Richardson; Chestertown, Eastern Shore, Maryland, John Bolton; Queenstown, Maryland, James Browne, James Kent, William Richmond and R. Wilson; Talbot, Maryland, John Nesmyth and William McCallum; Alexandria, Virginia, Josiah Watson and Robert McCrea; Dumfries, Virginia, Richard Graham; Fredericksburg, Virginia, William Smith; Newcastle, Virginia, F. Tate; Petersburg, Virginia, William Bradley; Suffolk, Virginia, John Driver; Aylett's Warehouse, Virginia, —— Pollard; Port Royal, Virginia, George Tankerslie; Yorktown, Virginia, Richard Brown; Bathtown, North Carolina, William Brown; Edenton, North Carolina, William Gardner; Wilmington, North Carolina, John Dubois; Georgetown, South Carolina, Robert Gibson and William Steuart; Jacksonburg, South Carolina, John Tod; Charleston, South Carolina, Peter Bonetheau; Purysburg, South Carolina, Frederick Rehm; Pocotaligo, South Carolina, Richard Wayne. Many of these individuals had already acted as postmasters at one time or another before the commencement of the Revolution, either with the Royal Mail or in Goddard's newspaper service, so that it was not an entirely untrained force that managed the various post-office stations.

In addition to the above names there are those of Richard N. Stephens, Surveyor for the Southern District; James Bryson, Surveyor for the Middle District; Alexander Purdie, who seems to have acted as an accountant; John Clarkson, who acted in a similar capacity; and Joel Erpin, Richard Cogdell, Thomas McLeane, William Brown, Richard Yorke, John Perkins, and John Bolton, whose duties are not defined. The express or post-riders of 1776 of whom there is record are: John King, Bernard Wolfe, E. Adams, Hugh M'Clenaghan, John Avery, Jr., Elijah Bennett, William Chew, Josiah Fessenden, Joseph Beck, and John Pluckrose.

In October, 1776, occurred the first mail mishap of which we have record. The important dispatches between Congress and the army were sent by special expresses, independent of the regular mail routes and schedules (Elijah Bennett and Josiah Fessenden seem to have been the most trusted of these); one of the riders was robbed of dispatches from General Washington, at Bristol, Pennsylvania. He was promptly arrested and a committee of Congress investigated the affair. The postmaster at Bristol was discharged for complicity in the theft; the express rider was imprisoned, but afterwards was cleared. The experience Congress gained in this investigation led to the Postmaster-General obtaining full control over the special expresses, and the incident has value mainly in showing that Congress thus early awoke to the expediency of leaving the civil bureaus as unhampered in the management of their affairs as the military officers were left unhampered in the management of the army.

Near the end of the year Benjamin Franklin was appointed Commissioner to represent the United States at the Court of France, and Richard Bache was selected to succeed him as Postmaster-General.

Political patronage, in the scramble for postmasterships, may be said to date from the beginning of Postmaster-General Bache's administration. Envy, masked as patriotism, represented to Congress in January, 1777, that persons disaffected to the American cause were employed as postmasters and riders. Congress called for a list of the names of employees and copies of their recommendations and, as there appeared to be reason why the Post-Office should be criticized, a thing that Benjamin Franklin's management escaped, asked pointedly why the regulations of the Post-Office were not carried out. Bache did not furnish the names as requested, but stated generally that every precaution had been taken at the first establishment of the Post-Office to prevent the employment of Loyalists. The Surveyors had been ordered to request the town committees or State conventions to nominate the postmasters and riders. In the appointment of deputy postmasters and post-riders these recommendations were made the rule of selection.

But one rider was dismissed as a result of this spasm of patriotism and the Postmaster-General stated that he was not entirely certain of the truth of the charge even in this case. The dismissal, therefore, was put upon the grounds of dilatory habits, of which evidence could be produced.

Protests of underpaid employees had been heard in 1777 and were heard again in March, 1778. Jonathan Hastings, postmaster at Cambridge and Boston, complained that the twenty per cent allowance was not sufficient, and after more complaint to the same effect, from others, Congress gave the Postmaster-General authority to grant an additional allowance, not to exceed two hundred dollars annually, to postmasters when, in his discretion, it appeared absolutely necessary.

Two additional Surveyors of the Post-Office were authorized during the year 1778 and the inspection tours were defined as from Casco Bay, then Massachusetts, to Philadelphia; from Philadelphia to Edenton, North Carolina; and from Edenton, to Savannah,

Georgia. An Inspector of Dead Letters was created and the inspectorship conferred on Ebenezer Hazard, whose duties were specified with such painful precision that it speedily became apparent they could not be performed by any one man. By means of this office, however, intelligence of considerable value found its way to Congress.

Near the end of 1777 it was found that the expense deficit of the Post-Office had greatly increased, and the postage rates were raised fifty per cent in an effort to meet the situation. The expense account of the Post-Office establishment, as balanced from the time Franklin relinquished the office of Postmaster-General to October, 1778, amounted, in round numbers, to thirteen thousand pounds. In 1777 the post-office at Philadelphia turned in the greatest amount of money for postage paid, with Baltimore, Albany, Annapolis, Boston, and Dumfries next, in the order named. The last quarter for 1778, and indeed for the year and a half preceding January, 1779, the post-offices showing the greatest returns in postage amounts collected were: Philadelphia; Easton, Maryland; Middletown, Connecticut; and Providence, Rhode Island. In January, 1779, the expense of the mail-rider service was eight times as much as it had been in 1776.

The personnel of the Post-Office Department at the end of the year 1778 was as follows: Postmaster-General, Richard Bache; Surveyor-General, Eastern District, Ebenezer Hazard; for the Middle District,

James Bryson; for the Southern District, Richard N. Stephens. Hazard, as before stated, was also Inspector of Dead Letters; Peter Baynton, the postmaster at Philadelphia, had been appointed to succeed Bache as Comptroller and Secretary, and Samuel Loudoun had succeeded Hazard as postmaster at Fishkill, New York.

In January, 1779, the Post-Office was thirteen hundred pounds and two years' salary in debt to the Postmaster-General. In April it raised the Postmaster-General's pay to two thousand dollars, but as that official still complained of its inadequacy it was raised to five thousand dollars at the end of the year.

A view of the general mail conditions in 1779 is given in Ebenezer Hazard's long letter of December 2, 1779, in which he sets forth the many difficulties under which the Post-Office labored. A principal cause of trouble was the grievance felt by the regular mail-riders because of the preferential treatment, both as to pay and rations, received by the special expresses. The current belief among the mail-riders was that the expresses received twenty dollars a day, and that they were paid, while in service, whether they were riding or not; they did draw both rations and forage from the public stores and none of their rides exceeded twenty miles. They carried letters privately, on which postage should be paid, and often attended to their private concerns while on public business. Hazard told, with righteous indignation, of an express

who offered a post-rider fifteen dollars to carry his
dispatches to the next station, on the very flimsy excuse that he could not find his horse. The expresses
seldom had more than a few single letters to carry,
and Hazard suggested that they transport the army
returns, which were being sent through the post-office
on frank. These valuable papers could easily be stolen
from the mail and the enemy gain important knowledge therefrom. They accumulated in the post-office
until sometimes there was a wheelbarrow load of them
before they could be sent off. The expresses, it
seemed, were promptly paid their handsome salaries
while the mail-riders were allowed a mere pittance
and even that was not regularly paid to them. This
letter from Hazard proved the proverbial last straw
with Congress which, at the end of the month, made a
sweeping revision of the express service by legislating
it out of existence; a remedy that merely substituted
for one set of evils another of a different type. The
expresses were abolished December 27, 1779, and the
protest from General Washington was prompt and
vigorous. The matter was compromised by granting
the Commander-in-Chief authority to employ expresses when he judged proper. This authority was
given January 14, 1780. A year later (December,
1781) the express service having again grown to
former proportions, all expresses were again dismissed, with the same proviso as before.

At the end of 1779, the postal rate was changed to

twenty-five "prices" above that of 1775 in an effort to meet the expenditures for the Post-Office establishment which amounted, in round numbers, to $111,970.

The Surveyors' traveling expenses were another exasperating difficulty. With the cost of everything steadily mounting and the value of the Continental dollar steadily sinking, these men, who were continually on the move throughout the Colonies, found great difficulty in fulfilling their duties. Congress tried the experiment, in January, 1780, of allowing the Surveyors their reasonable expenses instead of the forty dollars a day previously allowed them. But from the expense totals that came in under this arrangement, the Surveyors appeared to have forgotten the meaning of the word reasonable and, in May, the allowance was canceled and the postage rates doubled. The line from Philadelphia to Talbot, Maryland, was abolished and an effort made to secure revenue from the foreign mail, or "ships' letters," as they were called. These were ordered deposited in the post-office immediately on arrival. The sea captains had been very casual about the letters entrusted to them for delivery in the United States; no postage was paid upon them, and they were handed to almost any traveler for delivery. By this means a no inconsiderable loss to the Post-Office resulted and penalties were established to prevent the captains from sending forward their letters by private messengers.

Congress attempted to meet the expense of the

Post-Office by authorizing the Postmaster-General to draw warrants against the Continental Loan Offices of Massachusetts, Pennsylvania, Virginia, and North Carolina to a total that, among them, would amount to one hundred thousand dollars. This would have been a sensible bit of finance but for the fact that Congress drew so often and so extensively upon the Loan Offices for miscellaneous amounts that the important question was, Did these officers have the money? One phase of the Post-Office management by Congress was the continual jugglery of financial expedients to meet the departmental expense. The pay of officials and employees was raised and reduced, schemes were adopted, tried a few weeks or a few months and discarded, allowances were cut off, replaced, and then abolished until it is a marvel that any organization at all was maintained.

The Southern mail reached Congress but once a week and the maintenance expense of this seemed out of all proportion to the result, so, having dismissed the expensive expresses, Congress shifted the burden to the already sorely harassed regular mail-riders, who were expected to bring in mail twice a week from as far south as Charleston and as far north as Boston. By August, 1780, the experiment of a biweekly mail was abandoned. The mail-rider's pay was doubled, but in December this imaginary extravagance was repented of and the amount put back to the old figures. There were some favored mail routes; but these were by accident rather than design. Among them was the stage that ended at Fishkill, New York. It was looked upon as choice, for the rider could stable his horse there in the public stable and get forage at cost from the Military Storekeeper. This was an item not to be despised when expense accounts and salaries were irregularly paid and depreciation caused loss between the time the account was rendered and the money received.

The dangers of the mail service were real and not a few during the war. Several riders were waylaid and captured by the British or Tories, and robbery of the mail by stealth, fraud, and violence was not infrequent. But if the troubles were many, the patriotism of most of the personnel was equal to the strain. The conditions of the country during the Revolution were such that the wonder is that there were so few mail losses rather than that there were so many.

The Post-Office, together with all the other Government departments, as well as the Continental Congress itself, suffered from the relaxed tension that came after the surrender of Yorktown in 1781. The war was over and victory had been won; that was the universal feeling however doubtful the issue really continued to be. The year of the surrender, the files of the Post-Office give us the names of the post-riders in the service, and they are worth repeating here, as their routes are also given. The three divisions of the country, under which the Colonies had functioned during the war, the Eastern, Middle, and Southern, were not so strictly defined, so far as the Post-Office was concerned, as for some of the other Government departments. The Eastern District comprised New England, New York, and New Jersey; the Middle, Delaware, Pennsylvania, Maryland, and Virginia; the Southern, North and South Carolina and Georgia. The riders for the Eastern District were James Martin, who rode from Philadelphia to Morristown; Reuben Chadwick, from Morristown to Fishkill; Daniel Ayres, Fishkill to Albany; Elisha Skinner and James Pratt, Fishkill to Hartford; David Hyde, Edward Adams, William Torrey, Peter Mumford, and Benjamin Mumford, Hartford to Boston; John Noble, Boston to Portsmouth; and Joseph Barnard, Portsmouth to Falmouth. The Middle District riders were: William Gilmore, Philadelphia to Annapolis; William McCallum, Annapolis to Fredericksburg; Reuben Ballard, Fredericksburg to Hobb's Hole; Gideon Bosher, Fredericksburg to Newcastle; Alexander Stuart, Newcastle to Petersburg; Josh Abraham, Newcastle to Williamsburg; John James, Williamsburg to Suffolk; John Cowling, Williamsburg to Portsmouth; and John Wright, Suffolk to Edenton. The only rider whose name is available for the Southern District is William Brown who rode from Edenton to Newbern.

In January, 1782, Richard Bache resigned and Ebenezer Hazard was appointed Postmaster-General in his place. The management of the Post-Office was hampered by a mass of conflicting regulations, and one of Hazard's first recommendations was that Congress revise and codify all the acts and resolves relating to the Post-Office. This was undertaken, but was postponed and delayed until it was May of the next year before a complete plan of postal regulations was finally agreed upon.

Hazard's understanding of the needs of the service had been gathered at first-hand on his inspection tours as Surveyor, and he did much to simplify and improve the organization. He was able to reduce the post-riding expense by a fair saving and to establish a route from Petersburg, Virginia, to Edenton, North Carolina, on an arrangement that kept the United States free from expense for the first year of its operation. During his administration a great many mail robberies took place, and the question of detailing light dragoons as an armed escort for the riders was considered. This plan was not generally adopted because the cavalrymen could not be spared for such service, and, because where it was tried, the trooper made more trouble than he gave aid, for he disdainfully refused to carry any of the mail, and his scorn did not add anything to the cheerfulness with which the mail-rider performed his duty.

The insufficiency of the pay and traveling expense money of the Surveyors continued to be a vexation in 1782. In that year, more than half the postmasters did not receive from their twenty per cent commission over five pounds a quarter, and, as if this pittance fee was a matter of prime importance to Congress, there was a wrangle over the point whether this paltry sum was to be paid in hard money (silver) or the almost worthless Continental paper. Disposal of the increasing quantity of dead letters also became a problem in Hazard's administration. This class of mail had been under his direct control before he became head of the postal service. He had reported the difficulties, but by the time he became Postmaster-General the number of accumulated dead letters had become so great as to make the further saving of them appear foolish, even to Congress. Information of value had been obtained from them; toryism had been discovered and evidence of food and other speculations divulged, though nothing had been done as a result of such disclosures. Hazard wished to destroy all dead letters except those of evident value; but this matter, like so many others in the civic administration, went over and was postponed.

The question of postage on outgoing letters to Europe also arose. The practice seemed to have been for the writer of such letters to carry them in person aboard ship, or send them thither by a friend, and to pay the captain of the ship a small fee to carry the missive across the sea. Hazard insisted that this practice be stopped and that every letter to Europe go through the post-office. The rate was fixed at one shilling for single letters and others in proportion. Here, as from the incoming letters from abroad, a tidy bit of postage revenue was lost by the United States. This matter came up again in 1783, and was then finally settled by a clever arrangement which will be duly mentioned.

The Post-Office was investigated by a committee of Congress in January, 1783, and Hazard's administration completely approved. The committee found that he had conducted affairs with the utmost industry and economy and also with due regard for the public convenience. A reduction of the franking privilege then possessed by the Government departments was proposed in the beginning of the year, as the mind of Congress was set upon the most rigid economy; but an investigation committee considered that it could not be accomplished without detriment to the public service. The committee felt convinced that the department heads would truly pay for all ingoing as well as outgoing mail which was of a private nature, and frowned upon a suggestion that the Post-Office authorities inspect the mail to determine the point

The first case of fraud perpetrated through the Post-Office occurred in the year 1783, the last year of the war. Mail robberies had increased in number, but most of them were of minor consequence like the one that occurred at Princeton, New Jersey. In this the thief evidently thought he was getting something of value and when he found it was only a bag of letters he threw it away without opening any of them; they were all recovered, little the worse for the experience. The fraud case was of a more serious character, reflecting as it did upon the honor of the Post-Office in protecting the letters entrusted to its care. A firm of merchants, with houses in Philadelphia and Baltimore, failed in business. One of the creditors in Philadelphia, with the connivance of other creditors, applied for the mail of the father-in-law of one of the Philadelphia merchants. A letter was handed out, and afterward, when the father-in-law himself applied for his mail, the wrongful delivery was discovered. A prosecution in the courts was expected by the conniving creditors, who had suspected dishonesty in the failure and had obtained the father-in-law's letter to substantiate their suspicions. Hazard recommended to Congress that the United States sue the man who had obtained the letter on misrepresentation, but no Government action appears to have been taken.

One special branch of the postal service was the post-office and postmaster with the Main Army. This postmaster traveled with the troops and shared all their inconveniences and hardships in the field. The cost of this service, which was maintained at Headquarters, was about one hundred dollars per month and the method of mail delivery had been for the mail-riders passing nearest to where the army happened to be to turn off from their regular route and deliver the mail to the army post-office. This method was changed toward the latter part of the year 1777. It was ordered in October of that year that the regular mail-riders pay no attention to the position of the army, but deliver all army mail to the post-office nearest; the postmasters at such point were authorized to hire special expresses to carry the mail to army Headquarters direct. There had always been difficulty in keeping a good man in the position of postmaster at Headquarters for any length of time, as the pay was quite low, ten dollars per month, with two rations a day and forage for two horses. Most of the men who held this position resigned because they had no rank or authority and found themselves considered on a par with the common soldier. There was no distinguishing uniform for the position, though one of the postmasters is known to have worn green clothes, probably of his own designing. In 1783, with the position vacant, Postmaster-General Hazard asked permission to fill it on the best terms he could, unhampered by pay restrictions. The Congressional method of arranging this was to take the position away from the direction of the Postmaster-General and assign it to the military pay-roll of the Paymaster-General, which presumably permitted it to be filled by the detail of a military man to the post. The list of names of men who filled this honorable position is not complete. Thus far we know Hugh Smith, Hugh Hastings, Baxter Howe, John Durham Alvey, and Samuel Loudoun.

The final regulation of the Continental Post-Office was made by Congress, March 11, 1783. It was, in effect, a consolidation of the various acts and resolves from July, 1775, to October, 1781. In general these regulations provided that the Postmaster-General was to have supervision over all mail matters and to appoint deputies as he saw fit. The deputy's pay was fixed, as before, at twenty per cent of the income of his post-office; mails were to be once a week, and such post-offices as were found unnecessary could be discontinued by the Postmaster-General; the Supervisors, or Surveyors were granted four dollars a day and travel expenses; all post-office employees were exempt from military service; no one but mail-riders and expresses was allowed to carry letters, and these riders and expresses were forbidden to carry anything other than mail. It was made a felony to rob the mail; letters from abroad must be deposited in the Post-Office and the rate for these was fixed at one penny per letter; the postage rate for domestic letters was fixed at the old Royal Mail amount, before the war commenced; the list of the dead letters was to be published; the Postmaster-General's salary was fixed at twelve hundred and fifty dollars and that of his clerk at eight hundred dollars a year. The franking privilege was repealed, but the Commander-in-Chief, heads of separate armies, and Congressmen were allowed to send their letters free. There was some discussion over this last, but here, as in the case of the

department heads, it was assumed that the Congress-
man would declare and pay for his private mail.

The Post-Office received its first real shock in this
last year of the war. Since 1776, whatever had been
its difficulties it was spared that of competition, and
now, with peace assured, two lines of packet ships
were established, one by the French Minister to sail to
France and one by private enterprise to sail to England. The Postmaster-General was wroth, and took
the stand that, if mail were allowed to go by these
packets without first passing through the Post-Office,
it would be an insult to the dignity of the United
States. The French packets were a novel institution
and the amount of mail they might carry was so small
that the Postmaster-General thought they need not
be seriously considered; but the English boats were a
different matter. The mail here was heavier and, by
the British regulations, the postage fees could be paid
either in England or America. Experience had proved
that such fees were seldom paid in England, and the
return was made to the United States where the fee
was then paid. The British packets would not deliver
mail to the United States Post-Office except on a receipt; such receipt made the United States responsible
for the mail with no means of collecting the unpaid
postage. This responsibility and the labor of handling
would cost America, it was estimated, three thousand
pounds annually. Refusal on the part of the United
States Post-Office to deliver such letters would raise a

clamor from merchants and others to whom the letters were addressed that would be detrimental to the postal service. Hazard received this mail and forwarded only such part of it as involved the least risk. He so notified Great Britain, and thereafter all the letters came as common "ship's letters," which were minus all postage for the voyage, but subject to the domestic rate from their port of arrival to destination. It was at this point that the Postmaster-General showed real genius. He allowed a gratuity of one ninetieth of a dollar for all letters from beyond the sea that were deposited in the Post-Office by the sea captains bringing them over. This was the first mail subsidy in the history of the United States Post-Office. If the captains declined this fee, it would be sent to the Society for the Relief of Masters of Vessels, their widows and children.

As soon as this became known, all letters were promptly turned in at the Post-Office and the bluff seamen declined to accept the fee. In a very short time over ninety pounds accumulated which was turned into the fund of the Society, and the grateful thanks of those who were helped by it was recorded in the public prints. The merchants were well pleased to have their letters punctually delivered, the sea captains were glad to contribute to such a charity, the postal regulations were obeyed, and everybody was made happy.

During the war the Post-Office was directed by a

Postmaster-General, a Comptroller, and three Surveyors; at the end of 1783 the postal establishment had been reduced to a Postmaster-General and one assistant, while the mail had grown heavier and the volume of business greatly increased. The postage rates for 1784 were established upon the zone system; eight pence for fifteen miles; sixteen pence for thirty miles; one shilling for forty-five miles; and one shilling eight pence for sixty miles. However reasonable this was in the old days of horseback and stage, since the advent of the fast railroad train it was long ago demonstrated to be impracticable and obstructionary for letters and first-class mail. It still continues as a relic of archaic understanding, in our parcel-post charges. Newspapers were carried fifty miles for eight pence, one hundred miles for sixteen pence, and two hundred miles for one shilling eight pence. The regulations provided that they must be wrapped so that the number of copies could be known, and if any letter was placed therein the letter postage rate would be assessed. A most interesting practice was the grant of the privilege of post free exchanges of one copy of a newspaper between publishers, over one stage of the post-routes. The cost of the contract between Philadelphia and New York for a mail every day in the summer and three times a week in the winter was four hundred pounds per annum, in 1784.

With the abolition by Congress in this year of the franking privileges that had been granted to the military during the war, the Revolutionary activities of the Continental Post-Office came to a logical close. The service continued throughout the trying period of 1784–89 and was virtually the only branch of the Revolutionary Government that held its existence intact during the transfer year of 1789, when the present Government under the Constitution went into operation. The Post-Office therefore is the real point of contact between the old Continental Government of the Confederation and our present United States.

XVIII

THE PERSONAL SEAL AND VISITING–CARD OF BYGONE DAYS IN AMERICA

SOCIAL forms, the things people always do, or what it is considered proper to do, have an undoubted interest for most of us. The habitual methods of social intercourse, even the minor forms, if they have not always influenced human development have frequently served to illustrate it with some exactness.

Among the minor forms possessing this interest may be counted the personal seal and the visiting-card. The exact origin of these is not entirely clear, but both are worthy of more than a passing glance. The personal seal, or signet, dates back to the time of the pyramids, and it probably was accountable in some measure for the art of heraldry. The visiting-card does not appear, among English-speaking people at least, until about the middle of the eighteenth century, and it is of much less respectable and substantial parentage. The seal was the product of necessity; the visiting-card evolved as hardly more than a convenience. The seal was devised as a substitute for lack of skill in writing. It acquired distinction by virtue of the authority of its owner, and its artistic development, as a symbol of power and authority, adds a touch of beauty and romance to every written document on which it appears. The value of the written record in ancient days depended entirely upon the stamp of authority upon it, and the rulers and masters of men, while experienced and dexterous of arm with the broadsword and battle-axe, lacked the delicate skill of hand required by the sensitive quill pen. Therefore, in lieu of a signature, the overlord placed his seal, or signet, upon his orders, agreements, and contracts. The character of this seal, as it was to stand for the individual, was fashioned to portray some well-known and distinctive personal quality or prowess, and herein is to be found the beginnings of heraldic art. The American Indian followed the same idea in distinguishing himself by name, but it is difficult to say whether, in this case, the custom was a mark of social development or of a retrogression from a higher civilization. This personal signet required careful guarding to prevent theft and fraudulent use and the safest way was for the owner to keep it constantly upon his person. It was soon found that the most convenient way for this was the finger ring, which not only reduced the risk of theft and loss to a minimum, but had advantages of serving as a display-badge of authority and an article of personal adornment at one and the same time.

There was something curiously fitting in binding, or sealing, the written word with a disc of fast-clinging, long-lasting substance such as were the old mixtures of beeswax and resin; it was as though the impermanent nature of the written word was strengthened and fortified by a more lasting symbol, and, certainly, the ancient seals possessed lasting quality, for the remnants of some of the black wax medallions that still cling to parchments, dating before the Columbian discoveries, are as hard as stone and bid fair to last as long again. At first all seals were pendent; that is, they were moulded upon a strip of parchment laced into and hanging from the document. As political states came into existence, seals were devised for them as the symbol of their written authority. These seals grew in size and impressive elaborateness and some of them were at least five inches in diameter. To protect these ornate creations they were encased in metal, wood, silver, and gold, carved and decorated according to the importance of the documents to which they were attached. These encased seals have become known among irreverent archivists of the present generation as "snuffbox" seals. The awkwardness of these heavy pendent symbols led gradually to the change in practice of affixing the seals of state directly on the document. This direct fixation meant the elimination of the reverse of the seal, and the practice accounts for the very few examples, now in existence, of the reverse of the Great Seal of the United States.

This chapter, however, is concerned only with the personal seals of individuals, and these, very early, were impressed directly upon the document instead of hanging pendent as did nearly all of the official seals.

The personal seal never degenerated to the point of being embossed upon the document itself, but bravely fought out its battle until it went down to defeat in disuse and vanished before suffering such degradation. The true personal seal, of course, follows closely the legitimate family record, and, from its original function of authentication, it passed into the stage of protecting letters from perusal *en route* to their destination. Some idea of the long years that elapsed, from the time of the development of manuscript on parchment and paper until the rulers and men of power generally were able to write, may be gathered from the fact that, long after the art of writing had become one of the well-established marks of the gentry, the personal seal was still necessary to give legal value to the signature. Even to-day the seal tradition lingers, for the printed forms for minor legal documents still make provision for the old seal custom by printing the word "Seal," or the letters L. S. (Legal Seal), enclosed in a printer's stock ornament at the end of the signature line.

The official seal of the state, the court, and other political organizations superseded and finally ousted the personal seal, just as the growth of organized community power ousted the personal power of the ruler and overlord and the personal seal found refuge in the humbler duty of protecting the written communication from prying eyes. This use has made it difficult to find choice examples, or many examples at all, of the seals of eminent personages, for, before the day of the envelope, letters were folded for sealing in suchwise that the seal was necessarily destroyed in opening them. Among the vast stores of historical letters in the Library of Congress there is yet to be discovered a perfect specimen of the well-known seal of Thomas Jefferson bearing the motto: "Rebellion to Tyrants is obedience to God." The seal here shown was used by Jefferson on a letter written in 1781. From such seals as have survived a few have been selected as fair examples of interest. The predominant color of the wax used was red, though occasionally other colors appear and at rare intervals a brown, gold-flecked wax is encountered.

In Colonial and Revolutionary times every man of affairs possessed a seal, and democracy was not, in all cases, pushed to the point of discarding the heraldic symbols of ancestry. Some few of the Revolutionary Fathers, like Madison, Marshall, Jefferson, and Gerry, contented themselves with simple monograms; but by far the greater number continued the emblematic signet to which they were accustomed. Washington used at least four different seal signets, two of them being the plain monograms shown and the other two being modifications of the well-known Washington coat-of-arms. A small seal, beautifully cut and measuring barely one half inch in its longest, vertical dimension, shows the familiar crest and shield with an encircling scroll, beneath which is

SOME REPRESENTATIVE SEALS

Washington's motto: "*Exitus acta probat.*" The larger seal with the crest and arms is minus the motto and shows a palm to the left which is not in the Washington bookplate. President James Madison contented himself with the simple monogram "JM" surmounted by a scroll bearing the motto: "*Veritas non verba magistri.*" President Millard Fillmore and Chief Justice John Marshall have monograms minus mottoes and all decoration; Elbridge Gerry, a Signer of the Declaration of Independence, and "Light Horse Harry" Lee used seals devoid of heraldic embellishment. Henry Clay used a crest; Michael Hillegas, the first Treasurer of the United States, combined a complicated cipher with heraldic ornamentation; John Jay clung to the family arms, and Stephen Girard, the Philadelphia merchant and philanthropist, was content with a plain cipher. John Ettwein, the Pennsylvania Moravian bishop, who did such good work among the army hospitals during the Revolution, adopted a distinctively religious design for his seal, that of the Lamb of God, bearing the banner and cross. Benjamin Franklin's seal, here shown, is taken from an official *visé* when Franklin was acting as United States Commissioner in France, in 1777. It is undoubtedly the correct Franklin seal, as the controversy regarding it has been authoritatively settled; the confusion in the matter is easy to trace, for there are many Franklin letters in existence bearing entirely different seals. The old diplomat apparently used any seal that happened to be at hand in sealing his letters, but no instance has come to our knowledge of an official document bearing other than the seal here shown Washington, too, apparently did not use the arms and crest seal to seal mere letters, but one of the simple monograms. But among all the tastes and ideas displayed in the designs of personal seals there is one deserving of special mention because of its touch of graceful sentiment, so characteristic of the French people. When Lafayette visited the United States in 1824, he left behind him his armorial shields and heraldic devices and used for his personal seal, all the while he was in America, a miniature profile head of his friend George Washington, surrounded by rays of glory. In almost every instance he impressed this upon black wax.

The difficulty in positively identifying seals is not slight, and it does not always follow that the seal upon a letter, or even that impressed upon a legal document opposite a signature, is the personal seal of the signer; as an instance, the seal here shown was used by General Daniel Morgan on a letter of 1781 and exactly the same seal appears on a letter of Lydia H. Sigourney, fifty years later. It is interesting to know that the figure of Hope leaning upon an anchor appealed as strongly to the hardy Virginia frontiersman as it did to the cultured New England poetess.

Before the days of envelopes, seals for communications through the post were necessities and stock seals were purchasable which were, however, devoid of symbol or design and had merely checkered surfaces to aid in more firmly impressing the wax. Where wax was not used, a round paper wafer, with adhesive, was substituted. During the Revolutionary War every requisition from Washington's Headquarters, calling for stationery supplies, included a quantity of these wafers. ·

The first known record of the visiting-card appears about the year 1750 when the dandy and young man of fashion religiously spent a part of his time at the gaming-table. The backs of playing-cards were then perfectly plain, the need of the decorated back, to prevent marking the cards for cheating, not having been seriously felt; so, when the gallant called upon my lady and she was not at home, the most convenient way of registering his call was to inscribe his name upon the plain back of one of these playing-cards of which, apparently, a number were always carried, and leave it for her. Thus it happened that leaves from "the Devil's picture-book" became the ancestors of to-day's visiting card. Numerous examples of these inscribed playing-cards exist, some of them bearing the signatures of distinguished ecclesiasts. From this social use of a gambling implement the practice soon developed of having a distinctive, individual, and ornamental card, and in this fad the size of the pasteboard increased, sometimes to more than six inches in length, clogged with paper lace and other decorative nonsense. But the card-makers ruined their own game by these ornamental extravagances and the calling-card quickly reduced itself to the approximate size of the card of to-day, minus all decoration and bearing only the plain engraved name. Before the Civil War there existed a certain vogue for an engraved fac-simile of one's signature, but this has now fallen gen-erally into disfavor. Diplomats, professional men, the military, and the clergy use the official title upon their cards, and our judiciary, some time ago, adopted the practice of prefixing the judicial honor with the civil "Mr." such as "Mr. Justice Story." The Chief Justice of the United States does not usually give his surname upon his card, nor was it the fashion for Cabinet officers to do so. During the Civil War, Sec-retary Gideon Welles's card read: "The Secretary of the Navy." The President of the United States being the highest dignitary in the land, both socially and officially, pays no calls. He is called upon, and these calls are not returned, either in person or by card. Few Presidents have submitted to this restriction, however, and the President goes where and when he pleases; but theoretically, at least, no calls are paid by him as President. He has need for a card, however, for many minor courtesies and gifts of flowers from the White House conservatories are accompanied by a card, a little larger than usual bearing the words, in engraved and robust script: "The President." Recent exigencies created also a simple card of small size with two lines of engraved script: "The President of the United States of America." This was used abroad, but only for the same purposes as the domestic card. The President, as President, does not have a visiting-card. Cards of one hundred years ago were sometimes gilt-edged and often very highly glazed affairs upon a hard-coated surface that stiffened the thin paper nearly into the consistency of thin metal.

The Library of Congress is unfortunate in not possessing a specimen of George Washington's visiting-card. It is of record as of the average size of to-day, with an elliptical border frame, apparently printed, not engraved thereon, within which the General signed his name. Mrs. Washington used a printed floral garland on which to sign her name. In the early days the use of the "Mr." was the exception rather than the rule; the cards of Henry Clay, Daniel Webster, Elbridge Gerry, Jefferson Davis, and John C. Breckinridge are all minus the complimentary title. John Quincy Adams was "Mr. Adams" in commonplace, engraved script; James Buchanan was "Mr. Buchanan" in a very beautiful, engraved block letter; Lewis Cass, James K. Polk, and Edward Everett (who wrote his card in a precise New England penmanship) were all Misters; F. E. Spinner, like others, had an engraved facsimile of his fantastic signature upon his card. The creation of this absurdity was due to the misconception that a complicated signature is difficult to counterfeit, when the direct opposite is true. Spinner had evolved this complication as a financier and developed it when Treasurer of the United States during the Civil War. He suffered for it when the necessity arose for signing several thousand financial papers within a narrow time limit; he barely escaped paralysis from the resultant strain.

The visiting-card, while not a real necessity, is still a most convenient bit of social mechanics, in society as organized to-day, and it bids fair to remain in our daily life for a long time to come; but it never has and never can attain the importance of the personal seal as a symbol of power and authority.

XIX

SOME WORDS OF WASHINGTON WHICH
APPLY TO-DAY

THAT history repeats itself is a platitude, and it is not
entirely complimentary to our social and political intelligence that the parallel between our present difficulties and the situation of the United States in the
five confused years that followed the Revolution and
preceded the adoption of the Constitution is uncom-
fortably close. Because of this parallel many of Washington's comments at that time have a remarkable
application to the present situation, and a careful
perusal of the extracts following, from his letters during the years 1784–87, will prove decidedly interesting. We are apt to pass Washington by when searching for guidance among the ideas of the Fathers, perhaps because of the trite, commonplace quality of his
statements. Lacking the alert, sensitive, trained intelligence of Jefferson and his graceful facility of expres-
sion, and minus the robust, native philosophy of
Franklin, with his pungent originality of statement,
Washington's stiff and rather platitudinous phrases
often interfere with the recognition of the clear
common-sense of his vision. We seem to "have heard
all that before" in reading his stilted and involved
sentences; but it may be remembered that the Con-

stitution, some of the United States Statutes-at-Large, and even the Decalogue are in this class, yet they have not lost vitality by repetition.

In 1776, five days before the battle of Trenton, Washington wrote to the President of Congress:

> I have laboured, ever since I have been in the service, to discourage all kinds of local attachments and distinctions of country, denominating the whole by the greater name of AMERICAN, but have found it impossible to overcome prejudice.

Two weeks after resigning his commission at the close of the war, he wrote to Trumbull, one of his old aides-de-camp:

> Notwithstanding the jealous and contracted temper which seems to prevail in some of the States, yet I cannot but hope and believe that the good sense of the people will ultimately get the better of their prejudices; and that order and sound policy, though they do not come as soon as one would wish, will be produced from the present unsettled and deranged state of public affairs.

This unsettled and deranged state of affairs came with the close of the Revolutionary War, the departure of the British forces, and the disbandment of the Continental Army. The driving necessity of organized resistance to the armed forces in their midst no longer held the States to their more or less grudging team-work in the loose harness of the Articles of Confederation, and the result was a practical collapse of such power of centralized government as had, up to

then, existed in the United States. Then, as now, a
series of political and economic conditions, the result
of war, had developed without any reference to the
established frame of government, and, though our
Constitution to-day may be found adequate, Washington's analysis of the situation in the past, under
the Articles of Confederation, applies, not inaptly, to
much in the present. His criticism of the prejudice
and selfishness, of the slowness to recognize dangerous
conditions, of the tendency to look lightly upon public
faith, disinclination to deal justly with real grievances, worthlessness of newspaper reports, and the
greed for political power are fully as applicable in 1921
as they were in 1786.

He wrote to Benjamin Harrison, January 18, 1784:

That the prospect before us is, as you justly observe, fair,
none can deny; but what use we shall make of it is exceedingly problematical: not but that I believe all things will
come right at last, but like a young heir, come a little pre-
maturely to a large inheritance we shall wanton and run
riot until we have brought our reputation to the brink of
ruin, and then like him will have to labor with the current
of opinion, when compelled to do what prudence and common policy pointed out as plain as any problem in Euclid
in the first instance.

To Governor Trumbull he wrote in May:

Is it possible, after this, that it [the federal government]
should founder? Will not the All-wise and All-powerful
Director of human events preserve it? I think He will. He
may, however (for some wise purpose of His own), suffer

our indiscretions and folly to place our National character
low in the political scale; and this, unless more wisdom and
less prejudice takes the lead in government, will most
certainly happen.

Until October, 1786, when the news of Shays's Rebellion in Massachusetts reached him, Washington's
letters present, almost progressively, an excellent description of the condition of America. They are here
given with as little interference of reference as possible:

This . . . country . . . with a little political wisdom . . .
may become equally populous and happy. Some of the
States having been misled, ran riot for awhile, but they are
recovering a proper tone again, & I have *no* doubt, but that
our federal constitution will obtain more consistency &
firmness every day. We have indeed so plain a road before
us, that it must be worse than ignorance if we miss it. (To
Sir Edw. Newenham, June 10, 1784.)

As our population increases, and the government becomes more consistent; without the last of which, indeed,
anything may be apprehended, it is much to be regretted
that the slow determinations of Congress involve many
evils — 'tis much easier to avoid mischiefs than to apply
remedies when they have happened.   (To J. Read of S.C.,
August 11 and November 3, 1784.)

Some accounts say, that matters are in train for an ac-
commodation between the Austrians and the Dutch. If so,
the flames of war may be arrested before they blaze out
and become very extensive; but, admitting the contrary, I
hope none of the sparks will light on American ground,
which, I fear, is made up of too much combustible matter
for its well being. (To W. Gordon, March 8, 1784.)

With respect to ourselves, I wish I could add, that as much wisdom has pervaded our councils; as reason & common policy most evidently dictated; but the truth is the people must *feel* before they will *see*, consequently are brought slowly into measures of public utility. (To G. W. Fairfax, June 30, 1785.)

My first wish is to see this plague [war] to mankind banished from off the earth, and the sons and daughters of this world employed in more pleasing and innocent amusements, than in preparing implements and exercising them for the destruction of mankind. Rather than quarrel about territory, let the poor, the needy, the oppressed of the earth, and those who want land, resort to the fertile plains of our western country, the *second land of promise*, and there dwell in peace, fulfilling the first and great commandment. . . . [Washington's meaning was "Increase and Multiply" as he so states in a similar sentence in a letter to Lafayette this same day] . . . It is to be regretted that local politics and self-interested views obtrude themselves into every measure of public utility; but to such characters be the consequences. (To D. Humphreys, July 25, 1785.)

It is to be regretted, I confess, that Democratical States must always *feel* before they can *see:* — it is this that makes their Governments slow — but the people will be right at last. (To Lafayette, July 25, 1785.)

Ignorance and design are productive of much mischief. The first are the tool of the latter, and are often set to work suddenly and unexpectedly. (To R. H. Lee, August 22, 1785.)

A fair field is presented to our view; but I confess to you freely, my dear sir, that I do not think we possess wisdom or justice enough to cultivate it properly. Illiberality, jealousy and local policy mix too much in our public councils for the good government of the Union. . . . That we have it in our power to become one of the most respectable nations on earth, admits, in my humble opinion, of no doubt, if we could but pursue a wise, just and liberal policy towards one another, and keep good faith with the rest of the world. That our resources are ample and are increasing, none can deny; but, while they are grudgingly applied, or not applied at all, we give a vital stab to public faith, and shall sink, in the eyes of Europe, into contempt. (To J. Warren, October 7, 1785.)

The proposition in my opinion, is so self-evident that I confess I am unable to discover wherein lies the weight of objection to the measure [the proposed regulation of commerce]. We are either a united people or we are not so. If the former, let us in all matters of general concern, act as a nation which has a national character to support; if we are not, let us no longer act a farce by pretending to it; for, whilst we are playing a double game, or playing a game between the two, we *never* shall be consistent or respectable, but *may* be the dupes of some powers, and the contempt assuredly of all. . . . It is much to be wished that public faith may be held inviolable. Painful it is, even in thought, that attempts should be made to weaken the bands of it. It is a most dangerous experiment. Once slacken the reins, and the power is lost. It is an old adage that *honesty is the best policy.* This applies to public as well as private life, to States as well as individuals. (To Madison, November 30, 1785.)

My opinion is that there is more wickedness than ignorance in the conduct of the States, or, in other words, in the conduct of those who have too much influence in the government of them; and until the curtain is withdrawn, and the private views and selfish principles, upon which these

men act, are exposed to public notice, I have little hope of
amendment without another convulsion. (To H. Lee,
April 5, 1786.)

There are errors in our national government which call
for correction: loudly I would add; but I shall find myself
happily mistaken if the remedies are at hand. We are certainly in a delicate situation; but my fear is, that the people
are not yet sufficiently *misled* to retract from error. To be
plainer, I think there is more wickedness than ignorance
mixed in our councils. . . . Ignorance and design are difficult to combat. Out of these proceed illiberal sentiments,
improper jealousies, and a train of evils which oftentimes
in republican governments must be sorely felt before they
can be removed. The former, that is, ignorance, being a fit
soil for the latter to work in, tools are employed by them
which a generous mind would disdain to use; and which
nothing but time, and their own puerile or wicked produc-
tions can show the inefficiency and dangerous tendency of.
I think often of our situation, and view it with concern.
From the high ground we stood upon, from the plain path
which invited our footsteps, to be so fallen! so lost! it is
really mortifying. But virtue, I fear, has in a great degree,
taken its departure from our land, and the want of a dis-
position to do justice is the source of national embarrass-
ments; for, whatever guise or colorings are given to them,
this I apprehend is the origin of the evils we now feel and
probably shall labor under for some time yet. (To Jay,
May 18, 1786.)

Your sentiments that our affairs are drawing rapidly to
a crisis, accord with my own. What the event will be, is
also beyond the reach of my foresight. We have errors to
correct. We have probably had too good an opinion of
human nature in forming our confederation. . . . It is too
much to be feared, as you observe, that the better kind of

people, being disgusted with the circumstances, will have their minds prepared for any revolution whatever. We are apt to run from one extreme to the other. To anticipate and prevent disastrous contingencies would be the part of wisdom and patriotism. . . . I am told that even respectable characters speak of a monarchical form of government without horror. From thinking proceeds speaking; from thence to acting is often but a single step. But how irrevocable and tremendous! . . . What a triumph for the advocates of despotism to find that we are incapable of governing ourselves, and that the systems founded on the basis of equal liberty are merely ideal and fallacious! Would to God, that wise measures may be taken in time to avert the consequences we have but too much reason to apprehend. . . . I cannot feel myself an unconcerned spectator. Yet, having happily assisted in bringing the ship into port, and having been fairly discharged, it is not my business to embark again on a sea of troubles. Nor could it be expected that my sentiments and opinions would have much weight on the minds of my countrymen. They have been neglected, though given as a last legacy in the most solemn manner. [Circular letter to the governors of the States on disbanding the army, June 11, 1783.] I had then perhaps some claims to public attention. I consider myself as having none at present. (To Jay, August 1, 1786.)

In 1786 the economic depression of the country due to inefficiency, mismanagement, and profiteering during the war reached a climax of armed violence in Massachusetts. Debts, financial stringency, taxation, the condition of the farmers, the courts, and other equally familiar grievances to-day found a rallying-point and a leader in the person of Daniel Shays. The Massachusetts Legislature, after the usual hesitant

delay of democratic assemblies, finally passed three
different laws for easing the burdens of the people, but
the spirit of revolt had moved more swiftly and the
outburst came before the legal easement was felt.
The news reached Washington in October and drew
from him an outburst of shocked amazement:

For God's sake tell me what is the cause of these commotions? Do they proceed from licentiousness, British
influence disseminated by the Tories, or real grievances
which admit of redress? If the latter, why were they delayed until the public mind had become so agitated? If
the former, why are not the powers of government tried at
once? It is as well to live without, as not to live under their
exercise. Commotions of this sort, like snowballs, gather
strength as they roll, if there is no opposition in the way to
divide and crumble them. (To D. Humphreys, October 22,
1786.)

The picture you have exhibited and the accounts which
are published of the commotions and temper of numerous
bodies in the Eastern States are equally to be lamented and
deprecated. They exhibit a melancholy proof of what our
transatlantic foe has predicted; and of another thing perhaps, which is still more to be regretted, and is yet more
unaccountable, that mankind, when left to themselves, are
unfit for their own government. I am mortified beyond ex-
pression when I view the clouds that have spread over the
brightest morn that ever dawned upon any country. In a
word I am lost in amazement when I behold what intrigue,
the interested views of desperate characters, ignorance and
jealousy of the minor part, are capable of effecting, as a
scourge on the major part of our fellow citizens of the
Union; for it is hardly to be supposed that the great body
of the people, though they will not act, can be so short

sighted or enveloped in darkness, as not to see the rays of a distant sun through all this mist of intoxication and folly.

You talk, my good sir, of employing influence to appease the present tumults in Massachusetts. I know not where that influence is to be found, or, if attainable, that it would be a proper remedy for the disorders. *Influence* is no *government.* Let us have one by which our lives, liberties and properties will be secured, or let us know the worst at once. Under these impressions my humble opinion is that there is a call for decision. Know precisely what the insurgents aim at. If they have *real* grievances, redress them if possible; or acknowledge the justice of them, and your inability to do it at the present moment. If they have not, employ the force of government against them at once. If this is inadequate, *all* will be convinced, that the superstructure is bad or wants support. To be more exposed in the eyes of the world, and more contemptible than we already are, is hardly possible. To delay one or the other of these, is to exasperate on the one hand, or to give confidence on the other, and will add to their numbers; for, like snowballs, such bodies increase by every movement, unless there is something in the way to obstruct and crumble them before the weight is too great and irresistible.

These are my sentiments. Precedents are dangerous things. Let the reins of government then be braced and held with a steady hand, and every violation of the Constitution be reprehended. If defective, let it be amended, but not suffered to be trampled upon whilst it has an existence. (To H. Lee, October 31, 1786.)

Without an alteration in our political creed the superstructure we have been seven years in raising, at the expense of so much treasure and blood, must fall. We are fast merging to anarchy and confusion. . . . Will not the wise and good strive hard to avert this evil? Or will their supineness suffer ignorance and the arts of self-interested, designing, disaffected and desperate characters to involve this country in wretchedness and contempt? What stronger evidence can be given of the want of energy in our government than these disorders? If there is not power in it to check them, what security has a man for life, liberty or property? (To Madison, November 5, 1786.)

It is with the deepest and most heartfelt concern I perceive by some late paragraphs extracted from the Boston papers, that the insurgents of Massachusetts far from being satisfied with the redress offered by their General Court, are still acting in open violation of law and government and have obliged the chief magistrate in a decided tone to call upon the militia of the State to support the Constitution. What, Gracious God, is man, that there should be inconsistency and perfidiousness in his conduct? It is but the other day that we were shedding our blood to obtain the constitutions of our own choice and making; and now we are unsheathing the sword to overthrow them. . . . Keep me advised. Newspaper paragraphs unsupported by other testimony are often contradictory and bewildering. At one time these insurgents are spoken of as a mere mob; at other times as systematic in all their proceedings. . . . If the latter, there are surely men of consequence and ability behind the curtain, who move the puppets. . . . Influenced by dishonest principles [they] had rather see the country in the horrors of civil discord, than do what justice would dictate to an honest mind. . . . That the federal government is nearly if not quite at a stand, none will deny. The first question then is shall it be annihilated or supported? If the latter, the proposed Convention is an object of first magnitude and should be sustained by all the friends of the present constitution. . . . Yet I would wish anything and everything essayed to prevent the effusion of blood, and to avert the humiliating and contemptible figure we are about to make in the annals of mankind. (To D. Humphreys, December 26, 1786.)

I feel, my dear General Knox, infinitely more than I can express to you for the disorders, which have arisen in these states. Good God! Who besides a Tory, could have foreseen, or a Briton predicted them? . . . When this spirit first dawned, probably it might have been easily checked. . . . There are combustibles in every State, which a spark might set fire to. . . . It has been supposed that the constitution of the state of Massachusetts was amongst the most energetic in the Union. May not these disorders then be ascribed to an indulgent exercise of the powers of administration? If your laws authorized, and your powers are equal to the suppression of these tumults, in the first instance, delays and unnecessary expedients were improper. These are rarely well applied; and the same causes will produce similar effects in any form of government, if the powers of it are not exercised. . . . If the powers are inadequate amend or alter them; but do not let us sink into the lowest state of humiliation and contempt, and become a byword in all the earth. (To Knox, December 26, 1786.)

The moment is important. If government shrinks or is unable to enforce its laws, fresh manœuvres will be displayed by the insurgents, anarchy and confusion must prevail, and everything will be turned topsy-turvy in that State, where it is not probable it will end. . . . That which takes the shortest course . . . in my opinion will, under present circumstances, be found best; otherwise, like a house on fire, whilst the most regular way of extinguishing the flames is contended for, the building is reduced to ashes. My opinion of the energetic wants of the federal government is well known. . . . Indeed after what I have seen, or rather after what I have heard, I shall be surprised at nothing; for, if three years since any person had told me, that there would have been such a formidable rebellion as exists, at this day against the laws and constitution of our

own making, I should have thought him a bedlamite, a fit
subject for a mad house. (To Knox, February 3, 1787.)

On the happy termination of this insurrection I sincerely
congratulate you, hoping that good may result from the
cloud of evils, which threaten not only the hemisphere of
Massachusetts, but by spreading its baneful influence
threaten the tranquility of other States. Surely Shays
must be either a weak man, the dupe of some characters
that are yet behind the curtain or has been deceived by his
followers; or, which may be as likely as anything perhaps,
he did not conceive there was energy enough in the government to bring matters to the crisis they have been pushed.
(To Knox, February 25, 1787.)

That many inconveniences result from the present form
[of government] none can deny. . . . But is the public mind
matured for such an important change as the one you have
suggested? . . . A thirst for power and the bantling, I had
like to have said monster, for sovereignty, which have
taken such fast hold of the States individually, will when
joined by the many whose personal consequence in the
control of State politics will in a manner be annihilated,
form a strong phalanx against it; and when to these the
few who can hold posts of honor or profit in the national
government are compared with the many who will see but
little prospect of being noticed, and the discontent of others
who may look for appointments, the opposition will be
altogether irresistible till the mass, as well as the more dis-
cerning part of the community will see the necessity.
Among men of reflection, few will be found, I believe, who
are not beginning to think that our system is more perfect
in theory than in practice; and that notwithstanding the
boasted virtue of America it is more than probable we
shall exhibit the last melancholy proof, that mankind are
not competent to their own government without the means

of coercion in the sovereign. Yet I would fain try what the wisdom of the proposed convention will suggest. . . . It may be the last peaceable mode of essaying the practicability of the present form without a greater lapse of time than the exigency of our affairs will allow. (To Jay, March 1, 1787.)

The suppression of these tumults with so little bloodshed is an event as happy as it was unexpected; it must have been peculiarly agreeable to you, being placed in so delicate and critical a situation. I am extremely happy to find that your sentiments upon the disfranchising act are such as they are; upon my first seeing, I formed an opinion perfectly coincident with yours, *vizt.*, that measures more generally lenient might have produced equally as good an effect without entirely alienating the affections of the people from the government; as it now stands, it affects a large body of men, some of them, perhaps, it deprives of the means of gaining a livelihood; the friends and connections of those people will feel themselves wounded in a degree, and I think it will rob the state of a number of its inhabitants, if it produces nothing more. (To B. Lincoln, March 23, 1787.)

Laws or ordinances unobserved, or partially attended to, had better never have been made; because the first is a mere nihil, and the second is productive of much jealousy and discontent. . . . If the delegates come to it [the coming Constitutional Convention] under fetters, the salutary ends proposed will, in my opinion, be greatly embarrassed and retarded, if not altogether defeated. I am desirous of knowing how this matter is, as my wish is that the Convention may adopt no temporizing expedients, but probe the defects of the Constitution to the bottom, and provide a radical cure, whether they are agreed to or not. A conduct of this kind will stamp wisdom and dignity on their proceedings, and hold up a light which sooner or later will have its influence. (To Madison, March 31, 1787.)

The call for the Convention to consider alteration of the Articles of Confederation, so as to render them "adequate to the exigencies of Government and the preservation of the Union," had been issued by the Continental Congress in February, 1787, and, as the news of this intended attempt to improve conditions spread through the communities, the country settled down to await the result. On May 8th, Washington, as a delegate from Virginia, set out for Philadelphia to attend the meeting of this Convention, which was destined to formulate the present Constitution of the United States.

THE END

INDEX